WITHDRAWAL

Afro-American Writers

GOLDENTREE BIBLIOGRAPHIES

In Language and Literature
under the series editorship of
O. B. Hardison, Jr.

Afro-American Writers

compiled by

Darwin T. Turner

North Carolina Agricultural and
Technical State University

APPLETON-CENTURY-CROFTS

Educational Division

New York   MEREDITH CORPORATION

Preface

THE FOLLOWING BIBLIOGRAPHY is intended for graduate and advanced undergraduate students of literature who desire a convenient guide to drama, fiction, and poetry by Afro-Americans and to scholarship about those writers. The listing is necessarily selective, but every effort has been made to include major works, with emphasis on those published during the twentieth century. The concern is with writers in the United States; black writers of other nations are included only if they are significant in American literature.

Although the focus is on literature and literary scholarship of Afro-Americans, it has seemed advisable to include references to such related topics as the historical and sociological backgrounds; art, music, journalism, and folklore; and critical studies of uses of Africans and Afro-Americans as characters in American literature. Because such references are supplementary, the listing is not exhaustive but representative of major works providing necessary background for the student of literature. For these supplementary references, as for the works of literature, literary history, and literary criticism, the general practice has been to list the most recent printing or edition. When it has seemed significant, attention has been directed to the original date of publication.

References are made to works by white scholars as well as black scholars, and no attempt has been made to distinguish one group from the other. On the other hand, anthologies and scholarly works prepared by Afro-Americans have been excluded if not relevant to this bibliography. For example, W. S. Braithwaite's annual anthologies have been omitted because they have no significance for a student of literature by Afro-Americans. Similarly, Benjamin Brawley's history of English literature, Braithwaite's life of the Brontës, Richard Wright's examination of Spain, and other such works have been excluded because they are not related to the life or culture of black people in America.

Some readers may question the inclusion, in a scholarly bibliography, of articles from popular magazines and encyclopedias. Nevertheless, these frequently constitute two important sources of information about Afro-American writers and their works. Other readers undoubtedly will believe that too many authors have been included in Section IV, "Afro-American Writers." Obviously, no attempt has been made to include every Afro-American who has published a book of fiction or poetry. On the other hand, there has been no automatic exclusion of a writer who published his own work. In general, the writers included are those who have already received critical or popular attention, and those whose work is representative because of historical, attitudinal, or stylistic reasons. When in doubt, the compiler has included a writer rather than risk omitting work that might have value for users of the bibliography.

Except when they constitute extremely valuable or the only available sources, the following types of references have been excluded:

Book reviews in newspapers and periodicals.
Short articles on minor points.
Brief references in general articles on literature.
Unpublished doctoral dissertations and masters' theses.
General histories of American literature.

In general, the compiler has attempted to steer a middle course between the brief lists of references included in the average textbook and the long professional bibliography in which significant items are often lost in the sheer number of references given. This bibliography should materially assist the student in his effort to survey a topic, write reports and term papers, prepare for examinations, and do independent reading. Attention is called to four features intended to enhance its utility:

(1) Extra margin on each page permits listing of library call numbers of often-used items.

(2) Extra space at the bottom of every page permits inclusion of additional entries.

(3) An index by author follows the bibliography proper.

(4) The index and cross-reference number direct the reader of the page and position on the page of the desired entry. Thus, in an entry such as

GROSS, Seymour L. "Stereotype to Archetype: The Negro in American Literary Criticism." See 1.13, the number 1.13 indicates that the entry referred to is on page 1, and is the 13th item on the page. Both page numbers and individual entry numbers are conspicuous in size and position so that the process of finding entries is fast as well as simple.

An asterisk following an entry indicates a work of special importance in the field. Other annotations that may conclude an entry are: (1) a dagger (†) to indicate the item is available as a paperback and that full details can be found in *Paperbound Books in Print;* (2) cross reference(s) to other entries in the bibliography in which the work cited is also included; (3) a phrase describing the subject of an allusive title. (Bibliography) is used to indicate that an entry includes a valuable bibliography.

The following symbols are used in the bibliography. In most instances a symbol, as given in the column at the left, is used to designate the title of a periodical, serial, or publisher.

AAAP&SS	Annals of the American Academy of Political & Social Science
ABR	American Benedictine Review
A Forum	African Forum: A Quarterly Journal of Contemporary Affairs
AL	American Literature
AME Church Review	
AMer	American Mercury
The American Collector	
AMR	African Methodist Review
AmS	American Scholar
AQ	American Quarterly
AR	Antioch Review
Arena	
ArF	Arkansas Folklore
ASch	American School
Asia	
ASp	American Speech
AtM	Atlantic Monthly
BA	Books Abroad
BAASB	British Association for American Studies Bulletin
BB	Bulletin of Bibliography
Bookman	
Book Week, New York Herald Tribune	
BosUS	Boston University Studies in English
Brief	
C	The Crisis
Carolina	Carolina Magazine
CathW	Catholic World

CE	College English
CEA	CEA Critic
CEJ	California English Journal
Century	
Chautauquan	
ChinL	Chinese Literature
ChiR	Chicago Review
CJF	Chicago Jewish Forum
Colorado Quarterly	
CLAJ	College Language Association Journal
Commentary	
Commonweal	
CR	The Critical Review
Critic	
Criticism	
CritQ	Critical Quarterly
Cross Currents	
CUF	Columbia University Forum
CurOp	Current Opinion
Daedalus	
Descant	
Dial	
Diogenes	
Discourse	
Dissent	
Drama	
Drama Cr	Drama Critique
Ebony	Ebony Magazine
EdCF	Écrits du Canada Français
EJ	English Journal
Encounter	
Esquire	
ESRS	Emporia State Research Studies
ETJ	Educational Theatre Journal
FH	Frankfurter Hefte
Fortnightly	
Forum	
Four Quarters	
Freedomways	
GaR	Georgia Review
Graduate Comment	
Harpers	
HC	The Hollins Critic
Horn Book	
Independent	
ISSB	International Social Science Bulletin
JAF	Journal of American Folklore
JASP	Journal of Abnormal and Social Psychology
JEGP	Journal of English & Germanic Philology
JNE	Journal of Negro Education

JNH	Journal of Negro History
JQ	Journalism Quarterly
JSH	Journal of Southern History
KFR	Kentucky Folklore Record
Letture	
Liberator	
LibQ	Library Quarterly
Life	
LitD	Literary Digest
LitR	Literary Review
Mainstream	
M&M	Masses & Mainstream
MAQR	Michigan Alumnus Quarterly Review
MASJ	Midcontinental American Studies Journal
MdF	Mercure de France
Messenger	
MidF	Midwestern Folklore
MissQ	Mississippi Quarterly
MJ	Midwest Journal
MJAF	Music Journal of American Folklore
MLQ	Modern Language Quarterly
ModA	Modern America
ModQ	Modern Quarterly
MQR	Michigan Quarterly Review
MR	Massachusetts Review
MTJ	Mark Twain Journal
MVHR	Mississippi Valley Historical Review
NALF	Negro American Literature Forum (Terre Haute, Ind.)
ND	Negro Digest
New Challenge	
NEQ	New English Quarterly
New Masses	
New Yorker	
NHB	Negro History Bulletin
NL	New Leader
NMQ	New Mexico Quarterly
NQ	Negro Quarterly
North American Review	
NR	New Republic
NS	Die Neueren Sprachen
NYFQ	New York Folklore Quarterly
NYRB	New York Review of Books
O	Opportunity: A Journal of Negro Life
Ohio History Quarterly	
Outlook & Independent	
PA	Présence Africaine
Palms	
Paru	
PBSA	Papers of the Bibliographical Society of America

People's Voice
Phylon
PMLA   Publications of the Modern Language Association
Poet Lore
Poetry
PopSc   Popular Science
PR   Partisan Review
Preuves
Progressive
PsyR   Psychoanalytic Review
PubW   Publishers' Weekly
Reporter
Revue Anglo-Américaine
La Revue Nouvelle
Revue Politique et Littéraire
RGB   Revue Génerale Belge
RLV   Revue des Langues Vivantes (Bruxelles)
RPol   Review of Politics (Notre Dame)
RS   Research Studies (Washington State Univ.)
Samtiden
S&S   School & Society
S&SR   Sociology & Social Research
SAQ   South Atlantic Quarterly
SatR   Saturday Review
Sch   Scholastic
SELL   Studies in English Literature and Language
                             (Kyushu Univ., Fukuoka, Japan)
SFQ   Southern Folklore Quarterly
SHR   Southern Humanities Review
SLJ   Southern Literary Journal
SocF   Social Forces
SoR   Southern Review (Louisiana State Univ.)
SouP   Southern Packet
Southern Literary Messenger
Southern Renascence
SoW   Southern Workman
SR   Sewanee Review
Survey
SurG   Survey Graphic
SUS   Susquehanna University Studies (Selingsgrove,
                             Pa.)
SWR   Southwest Review
TamR   Tamarack Review
TC   Twentieth Century
TCL   Twentieth Century Literature
TDR   The Drama Review
TempsM   Les Temps Moderne
TFSB   Tennessee Folklore Society Bulletin
ThA   Theatre Arts
Time

TQ	Texas Quarterly
Tri-Quarterly	
TSL	Tennessee Studies in Literature
TSLL	Texas Studies in Literature & Language
UKCR	University of Kansas City Review
UTSE	University of Texas Studies in English
VQR	Virginia Quarterly Review
WestR	Western Review
WF	Western Folklore
WLB	Wilson Library Bulletin
WoT	World Today
WSCL	Wisconsin Studies in Contemporary Literature
WVPP	West Virginia University Philological Papers
WWR	Walt Whitman Review
XUS	Xavier University Studies
YR	Yale Review
YULG	Yale University Library Gazette
ZAA	Zeitschrift für Anglistic und Amerikanistik (East Berlin)

Note: *The publisher and the compiler will be grateful for suggestions which may improve future editions of the bibliography.*

Contents

Aids to Research

Bibliographies

The following are books and articles primarily concerned with providing bibliographies. Other useful bibliographies are indicated in other sections of this work.

1   AMOS, Preston E. *100 Years of Freedom: A Selected Bibliography of Books about the American Negro.* Washington, D.C.: Assn for Study of Negro Life and History, 1963.

2   ARNETT, Benjamin W. *et al.* "Works by Negro Authors." *Report of the Commissioner of Education for the Year 1893–94.* Washington, D.C.: GPO, 1896, I, 1056–61.

3   BROWN, Warren, comp. *Check List of Negro Newspapers in the United States, 1827–1946.* Jefferson City, Mo.: Lincoln UP, 1946.*

4   CHAPMAN, Abraham. *The Negro in American Literature and a Bibliography of Literature by and about Negro Americans.* Stevens Point, Wis.: Wisconsin State UP, 1966.

5   DODDS, Barbara. *Negro Literature for High School Students.* Champaign, Ill.: National Council of Teachers of English, 1968.

6   DUBOIS, W. E. B. *A Select Bibliography of the Negro American.* 3rd ed. (Atlanta University Publications, X) Atlanta, Ga.: Atlanta U, 1905.*

7   DUMOND, Dwight L. *Bibliography of Antislavery in America.* Ann Arbor: U of Michigan P, 1961.

8   ELLIS, Ethel M. *The American Negro: A Selected Checklist of Books.* Washington, D.C.: Negro Collection, Howard U, 1968.

9   FOREMAN, Paul B. *The Negro in the United States: A Bibliography.* Stillwater, Okla.: Oklahoma A & M Col, 1947.

10   GORDON, Eugene. "The Negro Press." *AAAP&SS* CXL (November, 1928), 248–256.

11   GREEN, Elizabeth L. *The Negro in Contemporary American Literature: An Outline for Individual and Group Study.* Chapel Hill: U of North Carolina P, 1928.

12   GRINSTEAD, S. E. *A Select, Classified, and Briefly Annotated List of Two Hundred Fifty Books by or about the Negro Published during the Past Ten Years.* Nashville: Fisk U Library, 1939. (Mimeographed.)

13   GROSS, Seymour L. and John Edward HARDY, eds. *Images of the Negro in American Literature.* Chicago: U of Chicago P, 1966.†

14   HOMER, Dorothy R. *The Negro in the United States; a List of Significant Books.* 9th ed., rev. New York: New York Public Library, 1965.

15   HOMER, Dorothy R. and Ann M. SWARTHOUT. *Books about the Negro: An Annotated Bibliography.* New York: Praeger, 1966.

1 KAISER, Ernest. "The History of Negro History." *ND*, XVII (Feb., 1968), 10–15, 64–80.* See also 25.20.

2 KAPLAN, Louis. *A Bibliography of American Autobiographies.* Madison: U of Wisconsin P, 1961.

3 KESSLER, S. H. "American Negro Literature; a Bibliographic Guide." *BB*, XXI (1955), 181–185.

4 LASH, John S. "The American Negro and American Literature: A Checklist of Significant Commentaries." *BB*, XIX (Jan–Ap., 1947), 12–15, 33–36.*

5 LASH, John S. "The American Negro in American Literature: A Selected Bibliography of Critical Materials." *JNE*, XV (1946), 722–30.

6 LAWSON, Hilda J. "The Negro in American Drama (Bibliography of Contemporary Negro Drama)." *BB*, XVII (1940), 7–8, 27–30.

7 *A List of Negro Newspapers, Magazines, Trade Journals and Press Services in the United States.* Washington, D.C.: Bureau of Foreign and Domestic Commerce, 1930–37.

8 *A List of Negro Plays.* Washington, D.C.: WPA Federal Theatre Project, 1938.

9 LOCKE, Alain. *The Negro in America.* Chicago: American Library Assn, 1933.

10 MC PHERSON, James M. and Lawrence B. HOLLAND, eds. *The Negro in America.* Lincoln University, Pa.: Lincoln UP, 1966.

11 MILLER, Elizabeth W. *The Negro in America.* Cambridge, Mass.: Harvard UP, 1966.*†

12 *MLA International Bibliography.* (Pub. each May as annual supplement to PMLA.)*

13 *The Negro.* (Catalogue No. 83.) New York: University Place Book Shop, 1952.

14 *The Negro in Print: Bibliographic Survey.* Washington, D.C.: The Negro Bibliographic and Research Center, 1965. (Pub. every two months.)

15 *Negro Newspapers on Microfilm: A Selected List.* Washington, D.C.: Library of Congress, 1953.

16 PENN, Joseph E., and others. *The Negro American in Paperback; a Selected List of Paperbound Books.* Washington, D.C.: National Education Assn, 1967.

17 PORTER, Dorothy B. "Early American Negro Writings: A Bibliographical Study." *PBSA*, XXXIX (1945), 192–268.

18 PORTER, Dorothy B. *North American Negro Poets: A Bibliographical Check List of Their Writings, 1760–1944.* New York: Franklin, 1963. (Reprinted; originally published in 1944.)*

19 PORTER, Dorothy B. *A Selected List of Books by and about the Negro.* Washington, D.C.: GPO, 1936.

20 PORTER, Dorothy B. "Some Recent Literature Pertaining to the American Negro." *WLB*, IX (June, 1935), 569–70.

21 PORTER, Dorothy B. *A Working Bibliography on the Negro in the United States.* Ann Arbor, Mich.: University Microfilms, 1968.*

22 REDDEN, C. L. "The American Negro: An Annotated List of Educational Films and Film Strips." *JNE*, XXXIII (1964), 79–82.

23 ROLLINS, Charlemae. *We Build Together.* 3rd ed., rev. Champaign, Ill.: National Council of Teachers of English, 1967.†

1 SALK, Erwin A. *A Layman's Guide to Negro History.* Enlarged ed. New York: McGraw-Hill, 1967. [Ramparts.]*

2 SCALLY, Sister Mary Anthony. *Negro Catholic Writers 1900–1943; a Bio-Bibliography.* Detroit: Romig, 1945.

3 SCHOMBURG, Arthur A., comp. *A Bibliographical Checklist of American Negro Poetry. Bibliographical Americana,* Vol. II. Ed. C. F. Heartman. New York: Heartman, 1916.

4 THOMPSON, Edgar T. and Alma M. *Race and Region: A Descriptive Bibliography Compiled with Special Reference to the Relations between Whites and Negroes in the United States.* Chapel Hill: U of North Carolina P, 1949.

5 *Selected Bibliography on the Negro.* 4th ed. New York: National Urban League, 1951; supp., 1958.

6 WELSCH, Erwin K. *The Negro in the United States: A Research Guide.* Bloomington: Indiana UP, 1965.

7 WHITEMAN, Maxwell. *A Century of Fiction by American Negroes, 1853–1952.* Philadelphia: Jacobs, 1955.*

8 WOODRESS, James, ed. *American Literary Scholarship: An Annual, 1963–65.* Durham: Duke UP, 1965–67.

9 WORK, Monroe N. *A Bibliography of the Negro in Africa and America.* New York: Octagon, 1965. (Orig. pub., 1928.)

Guides to Collections

Many public and university libraries have collections. In addition to those named, particularly useful collections are at Fisk University and Tuskegee Institute.

10 *The Arthur B. Spingarn Collection of Negro Authors.* Washington, D.C.: Howard U, 1948. (The Spingarn Collection at Howard.)

11 BONTEMPS, Arna. "The James Weldon Johnson Memorial Collection of Negro Arts and Letters." *YULG,* XVIII (October, 1943), 19–26. (The Johnson Collection at Yale.)

12 BONTEMPS, Arna. "Special Collections of Negroana." *LibQ,* XIV (1944), 187–206.

13 *Catalogue, Heartman Negro Collection.* Houston, Tex.: Texas Southern UP, 1957.

14 *A Catalogue of Books in the Moorland Foundation.* Washington, D.C.: Howard U, 1939. (Mimeographed.) (The Moorland Collection at Howard.)

15 *A Classified Catalogue of the Negro Collection in the Collis P. Huntington Library.* Hampton, Va.: Hampton Institute P, 1940. (Mimeographed.)

16 *A Dictionary Catalog of the Schomburg Collection of Negro Literature and History.* 9 vols. Boston: Hall, 1962. (The Schomburg Collection in New York City Public Library.)*

17 LEWINSON, Paul. *A Guide to Documents in the National Archives for Negroes.* Washington, D.C.: American Council of Learned Societies, 1947.

18 *Lists of Books by and about Negroes Available in the Libraries of the University of North Carolina and Duke University.* Raleigh: U of North Carolina, n.d.

19 *Peabody Collection of Works by and about Negroes.* Hampton, Va.: Hampton Institute P, 1945. (Mimeographed.)

1   "A Rare Collection of Negro Literary Works." *NHB*, XXVII (April, 1964), 162–163.

2   WRIGHT, Dorothy. "Comprehensive Thesaurus of Literature by and on the Negro." *S&S*, LXIII (1946), 430–31. (The H. P. Slaughter Collection.)

Encyclopedias, Handbooks, and Other Reference Works

3   ADAMS, Russell L. *Great Negroes, Past and Present*. Chicago: Afro-American, 1964.

4   CULP, D. W. *Twentieth Century Negro Literature, or, a Cyclopedia of Thought*. . . . Naperville, Ill.: Nichols, 1902.

5   DAVIS, John P., ed. *The American Negro Reference Book*. Englewood Cliffs, N.J.: Prentice-Hall, 1966.

6   *Dictionary of American Biography*. New York: Scribner's, 1928–37; 1946; 1958. (Published under auspices of American Council of Learned Societies.)

7   *Directory of U.S. Negro Newspapers, Magazines, and Periodicals*, 1966. New York: U.S. Negro World, 1966.

8   DUBOIS, W. E. B. and Guy B. JOHNSON. *Encyclopedia of the Negro: Preparatory Volume*. Rev. ed. New York: Phelps-Stokes Fund, 1946.

9   EMBREE, Edwin R. *American Negroes, a Handbook*. New York: Day, 1942.

10   GUZMAN, Jessie Parkhurst, Lewis W. JONES, and Woodrow HALL. *Negro Year Book*. New York: Wise, 1952.

11   *International Library of Negro Life and History*. 10 vols. Washington: Associated Pub., 1967–69.

12   KUNITZ, Stanley and Howard HAYCRAFT, eds. *American Authors, 1600–1900: A Biographical Dictionary of American Literature*. New York: Wilson, 1938.

13   MURRAY, Florence. *The Negro Handbook*. New York: Malliet, 1942.

14   MURRAY, Florence. *The Negro Handbook, 1944*. New York: Current Reference Pub., 1944.

15   MURRAY, Florence. *The Negro Handbook*, 1946–47. New York: Wyn, 1947.

16   MURRAY, Florence. *The Negro Handbook*, 1949. New York: Macmillan, 1949.

17   *The Negro Handbook*, comp. by Editors of *Ebony*. Chicago: Johnson, 1966.

18   *The Negro Yearbook; an Annual Encyclopedia of the Negro*. Tuskegee Institute, Ala, 1912–52.

19   PLOSKI, Harry A. and Roscoe C. BROWN. *The Negro Almanac*. New York: Bellwether, 1967.

20   SALK, Erwin A. See 3.1.

21   SLOAN, Irvin J. *The American Negro: A Chronology and Fact Book*. Dobbs Ferry, N.Y.: Oceana, 1965.

22   WELSCH, Erwin K. See 3.6.

23   *Who's Who in Colored America*. New York: Who's Who in Colored America Corporation, 1927; 7th (and last) ed., 1950.

Periodicals Significant to Study of Literature by Afro-Americans

1　See 1.3, 2.7, 2.15.

2　*The College Language Association Journal.* Baltimore, 1957 to date. (3 issues annually to 1966; quarterly afterwards.)

3　*The Crisis; a Record of the Darker Races.* New York: Crisis Pub, 1910 to date. (Monthly; includes annual review of literature by Negroes.)

4　*Ebony.* Chicago: Johnson, 1945 to date. (Monthly; monthly review of popular works by and about Negroes.)

5　*Freedomways: A Quarterly of the Negro Freedom Movement.* New York: Freedomways Associates, 1961 to date. (Each issue includes a review of recent books.)

6　*A Guide to Negro Periodical Literature.* Winston-Salem, N.C.: Winston-Salem State Col., 1941–46.

7　*Index to Periodical Articles by and about Negroes.* Vol. XVII. Boston: Hall, 1967. (Formerly *Index to Selected Periodicals.*)

8　*Index to Selected Periodicals.* Vols. I–XVI. Boston: Hall, 1961–65.

9　*The Journal of Black Poetry*, #4, 1308 Masonic Ave., San Francisco, 1967 to date. (Quarterly.)

10　*The Journal of Human Relations.* Wilberforce, Ohio: Central State Col., 1952 to date. (Quarterly.)

11　*The Journal of Negro Education.* Washington, D.C.: College of Education, Howard U, 1932 to date. (Quarterly.)

12　*The Journal of Negro History.* Washington, D.C.: Assn for the Study of Negro Life and History, 1916 to date. (Quarterly.)

13　*Negro American Literature Forum.* Terre Haute: Indiana State U, Fall, 1967 to date. (Quarterly Newsletter.)

14　*Negro College Quarterly.* Wilberforce, Ohio: Central State Col., 1943.

15　*Negro Digest.* Chicago: Johnson, 1942–51, 1961 to date. (Monthly; monthly column on literature by and about Negroes.)

16　*Negro History Bulletin.* Washington, D.C.: Association for the Study of Negro Life and History, 1937 to date. (Monthly, October through June.)

17　*The Negro Quarterly: A Review of Negro Life and Culture.* New York: Negro Pub. Soc. of Am., 1945 to date.

18　*Opportunity: A Journal of Negro Life.* New York: National Urban League, 1923–1946. (Monthly; includes annual review of lit. by and about Afro-Americans.)

19　*Phylon: The Atlanta University Review of Race and Culture.* Atlanta, Ga.: Atlanta U, 1940 to date. (Quarterly; includes annual review of literature by and about Afro-Americans.)

20　PORTER, Dorothy B. and Ethel M. ELLIS. *Index to the Journal of Negro Education.* Vols. I–XXXI. Washington, D.C.: Howard U, 1953.

21　POUNCY, Mitchell L. *An Annotated Cumulative Index to Phylon Quarterly from 1950 through 1959.* Atlanta: Atlanta University School of Library Science, 1961. (Master's thesis.)

22　*Présence Africaine: Cultural Revue of the Negro World.* Paris and New York, 1947 to date.

1 *Quarterly Review of Higher Education among Negroes.* Charlotte, N.C.: Johnson C. Smith U, 1933 to date.

2 *The Southern Workman.* Hampton, Va.: Hampton Institute, 1872–1939. (Monthly.)

Backgrounds
Significant Autobiographies and Collections of Essays by Afro-Americans

The autobiographies listed here have been restricted to those by Afro-Americans distinguished in letters rather than in another field. The collections of essays have been designated by (Essays) following the entry. Additional collections of essays will be found in other sections of the bibliography. Each collection included in this section is a compilation by a single writer who has earned recognition as a literary artist. These essays have been singled out for readers who may wish to study the style as well as the thought.

3 BALDWIN, James. *The Fire Next Time.* New York: Dial, 1963. (Essays.)*†

4 BALDWIN, James. *Nobody Knows My Name.* New York: Dial, 1961. (Essays.)*†

5 BALDWIN, James. *Notes of a Native Son.* Boston: Beacon, 1955. (Essays.)*†

6 BARTON, Rebecca C. *Witnesses for Freedom; Negro Americans in Autobiography.* New York: Harper, 1948. (Summaries of autobiographies by Negro authors.)*

7 BENNETT, Lerone, Jr. *The Negro Mood.* Chicago: Johnson, 1965.†

8 BROWN, Claude. *Manchild in the Promised Land.* New York: Macmillan, 1965.*†

9 DOUGLASS, Frederick. *The Life and Times of Frederick Douglass.* New York: Pathway, 1941.*†

10 DOUGLASS, Frederick. *Narrative of the Life of Frederick Douglass, an American Slave.* Cambridge, Mass.: Harvard UP, 1960. (Originally published in 1845.)*†

11 DUBOIS, W. E. B. *Autobiography: A Soliloquy.* New York: International Pub., 1968.†

12 DUBOIS, W. E. B. *Dusk of Dawn.* New York: Harcourt, Brace, 1940.*†

13 DUBOIS, W. E. B. *The Souls of Black Folk: Essays and Sketches.* Chicago: McClurg, 1903; Blue Heron, 1953.†

14 ELLISON, Ralph. *Shadow and Act.* New York: Random, 1964.† (Essays.)

15 HENSON, Josiah. *The Life of Josiah Henson, ...* London: Gilpin, 1851. (Henson's autobiography reputedly provided H. B. Stowe with the model for Uncle Tom; the autobiography was last printed as *Truth is Stranger than Fiction,* Boston: Russell, 1879.)†

16 HUGHES, Langston. *I Wonder as I Wander.* New York: Rinehart, 1956.†

17 HUGHES, Langston. *The Big Sea.* New York: Knopf, 1940.*†

18 HURSTON, Zora Neale. *Dust Tracks on a Road.* Philadelphia: Lippincott, 1942.

19 JOHNSON, James W. *Along This Way.* New York: Viking, 1947. (Originally published in 1933.)*†

20 JONES, LeRoi. *Home: Social Essays.* New York: Morrow, 1966. (Essays.)†

21 KILLENS, John O. *Black Man's Burden.* New York: Trident, 1965. (Essays.)

22 MALCOLM X and Alex Haley. *The Autobiography of Malcolm X.* New York: Grove, 1965.*†

1 MC KAY, Claude. *A Long Way from Home.* New York: Furman, 1937.

2 REDDING, Saunders. *No Day of Triumph.* New York: Harper, 1942.

3 REDDING, Saunders. *On Being Negro in America.* Indianapolis: Bobbs-Merrill, 1951. (Essays.)*†

4 SCHUYLER, George S. *Black and Conservative: The Autobiography of George S. Schuyler.* New Rochelle, N.Y.: Arlington, 1966.

5 WASHINGTON, Booker T. *Up From Slavery.* New York: Doubleday, 1902.†

6 WILLIAMS, John A. *This Is My Country Too.* New York: New American Library, 1965. (Essays.)†

7 WRIGHT, Richard. *Black Boy; a Record of Childhood and Youth.* New York and London: Harper, 1945.*†

8 WRIGHT, Richard. *White Man, Listen!* New York: Doubleday, 1957. (Essays.)†

Slave Narratives

The following is a representative rather than a complete listing of slave narratives. Some of the narratives were ghost-written, but no effort has been made to identify these in the list. The narratives are included as guides to historical backgrounds rather than as models of literary achievement.

9 BIBB, Henry. *Narrative of the Life and Adventures of Henry Bibb, an American Slave.* New York: The Author, 1849.

10 BOTKIN, B. A., ed. *Lay My Burden Down: A Folk History of Slavery.* Chicago: U of Chicago P, 1945. (Collection of slave narratives.)†

11 BROWN, William Wells. *Narrative of William W. Brown, a Fugitive Slave.* Boston: Anti-Slavery Office, 1847.†

12 CLARKE, Lewis Garrard. *Narratives of the Sufferings of Lewis and Milton Clarke.* Boston: Marsh, 1848.

13 DOUGLASS, Frederick. See 6.9, 6.10.

14 GRANDY, Moses. *Narrative of the Life of Moses Grandy.* 2nd ed. Boston: Johnson, 1844.

15 LANE, Lunsford. *The Narrative of Lunsford Lane.* 3rd ed. Boston: Howes and Watson, 1845.

16 LOGUEN, Jermain Wesley. *The Rev. J. W. Loguen, as a Slave and as a Freeman.* Syracuse, N.Y.: Truair, 1859.

17 MELBOURN, Julius. *Life and Opinions of Julius Melbourn.* 2nd ed. Syracuse: Hall, 1851.

18 NICHOLS, Charles H. *Many Thousand Gone: The Ex-Slaves' Account of Their Bondage and Freedom.* Leiden, Netherlands: Brill, 1963. (Collection of slave narratives.)*

19 NORTHRUP, Solomon. *Twelve Years a Slave.* Buffalo: Derby, Orton, and Mulligan, 1853.

20 PENNINGTON, James W. C. *The Fugitive Blacksmith, or Events in the History of James W. C. Pennington.* 3rd ed. London: Gilpin, 1850.

21 *Slave Narratives.* Washington: Federal Writers' Project, 1941. (Folk history of slavery gathered from interviews with former slaves.)

22 STEWARD, Austin. *Twenty-two Years a Slave and Forty Years a Freeman.* Rochester: Alling, 1857.

23 VASSA, Gustavus. *The Interesting Narrative of the Life of Oloudah Equiano or Gustavus Vassa.* 2 vols. London, 1789.

Historical, Social, and Intellectual Backgrounds

Emphasis must again be placed upon the fact that the following is not an exhaustive list but a list of major works which should provide the necessary background for students of literature, for whom this bibliography has been prepared. A student of history or sociology will find the list useful but may desire a more complete compilation.

1 ADAMS, Russell. See 4.3.

2 APTHEKER, Herbert. *Nat Turner's Slave Rebellion.* New York: Humanities, 1966.†

3 APTHEKER, Herbert, ed. *A Documentary History of the Negro People in the United States.* 2 vols. New York: Citadel, 1951.*†

4 BAILEY, Harry A., Jr., ed. *Negro Politics in America.* Columbus, Ohio: Merrill, 1967.

5 BAKER, Ray S. *Following the Color Line: American Negro Citizenship in the Progressive Era.* New York: Harper, 1964. (Orig. pub., 1908.)†

6 BARBOUR, Floyd, ed. *The Black Power Revolt.* Boston: Extending Horizons, 1968.*†

7 BARDOLPH, Richard. *The Negro Vanguard.* New York: Rinehart, 1959.*†

8 BENNETT, Lerone, Jr. *Before the Mayflower: A History of the Negro 1619–1962.* Chicago: Johnson, 1962.†

9 BENNETT, Lerone, Jr. *Black Power U.S.A.: The Human Side of Reconstruction 1867–1877.* Chicago: Johnson, 1967.

10 BENNETT, Lerone, Jr. *Pioneers in Protest.* Chicago: Johnson, 1968. (Biographies.)

11 BENNETT, Lerone, Jr. See 6.7.

12 BERNARD, Jessie. *Marriage and Family among Negroes.* Englewood Cliffs, N.J.: Prentice-Hall, 1966.†

13 BERRIAN, Albert H. and Richard A. LONG. *Negritude: Essays and Studies.* Hampton, Va.: Hampton Institute P, 1967.

14 BOND, Horace Mann. *The Education of the Negro in the American Social Order.* New York: Octagon, 1966. (Orig. pub., 1934.)

15 BONTEMPS, Arna, ed. *Negro American Heritage.* San Francisco: Century Schoolbook, 1965.

16 BONTEMPS, Arna. *One Hundred Years of Negro Freedom.* New York: Dodd, Mead, 1961.*†

17 BONTEMPS, Arna. *The Study of the Negro.* New York: Knopf, 1948.

18 BONTEMPS, Arna and Jack CONROY. *Any Place but Here.* New York: Doubleday, 1966. (Originally published as *They Seek a City,* 1945.)†

19 BRAWLEY, Benjamin. *Negro Builders and Heroes.* Chapel Hill: U of North Carolina P, 1937.

20 BRODERICK, Francis and A. MEIER, eds. *Negro Protest Thought in the Twentieth Century.* Indianapolis: Bobbs-Merrill, 1965.†

1 BROOM, Leonard and Norval D. GLENN. *Transformation of the Negro American.* New York: Harper, 1965.†

2 BROWN, William Wells. *The Black Man: His Antecedents, His Genius, and His Achievements.* New York: Thomas Hamilton; Boston: Wallcut, 1863.

3 BROWN, William Wells. *The Rising Son; or The Antecedents and Advancement of the Colored Race.* Boston: Brown, 1873.

4 BUCKMASTER, Henrietta. *Freedom Bound.* New York: Macmillan, 1965.†

5 BULLOCK, Henry A. *A History of Negro Education in the South: From 1619 to the Present.* Cambridge: Harvard UP, 1968.

6 BULLOCK, Ralph W. *In Spite of Handicaps; Brief Biographical Sketches with Discussion Outlines of Outstanding Negroes Now Living....* New York: Associated Pub., 1927. (Bibliography.)

7 BUTCHER, Margaret. *The Negro in American Culture.* New York: Knopf, 1956. (Based on materials compiled by Alain Locke.)*†

8 CABLE, George W. *The Negro Question.* New York: Doubleday, 1958.†

9 CABLE, George W. *The Silent South.* New York: Scribner, 1885.

10 CARMICHAEL, Stokely and Charles V. HAMILTON. *Black Power: The Politics of Liberation.* New York: Random, 1967.†

11 "A Century of Struggle." *Progressive,* XXVI (Dec., 1962), 3–58. (Entire issue; essays by Baldwin, King *et al.*)

12 CHARTERS, Samuel B. *The Poetry of the Blues.* New York: Oak, 1963.†

13 CHESNUTT, Charles W. *Frederick Douglass.* Boston: Small, Maynard, 1899.

14 CLARK, Kenneth. *Dark Ghetto.* New York: Harper & Row, 1965.†

15 CLARK, Kenneth. *The Negro Protest.* Boston: Beacon, 1963. (Conversations with Baldwin, King, and Malcolm X.)

16 CLARK, Thomas D. *The Emerging South.* New York: Oxford UP, 1961.†

17 CLARKE, John Henrik. "Reclaiming the Lost African Heritage." See 21.10, pp. 21–27.

18 CLEAVER, Eldridge. *Soul on Ice.* New York: McGraw-Hill, 1968.*†

19 CORROTHERS, James D. *In Spite of the Handicaps.* New York: Doran, 1916. (Biographies.)

20 COTTER, Joseph S. *Negroes and Others at Work and Play.* New York: Paebar, 1947.

21 CRONON, E. D. *Black Moses: The Story of Marcus Garvey and the Universal Negro Improvement Association.* Madison, Wis.: U of Wisconsin P, 1955.†

22 CRUSE, Harold. *The Crisis of the Negro Intellectual.* New York: Morrow, 1967.*†

23 CULP, Daniel, ed. See 4.4.

24 DAVID, Leona King. "Literary Opinions on Slavery in American Literature from after the American Revolution to the Civil War." *NHB,* XXIII (1960), 99–103.

1 DAVIDSON, Basil. *Africa: History of a Continent*. New York: Macmillan, 1966. (Information about cultural heritage of first slaves.)*

2 DAVIE, Maurice. *Negroes in American Society*. New York: McGraw-Hill, 1949.

3 DAVIS, Allison W. and John DOLLARD. *Children of Bondage*. Washington, D.C.: American Council on Education, 1940.*†

4 DOBLER, Lavinia and Edgar TOPPIN. *Pioneers and Patriots: The Lives of Six Negroes of the Revolutionary Era*. (Phillis Wheatley, B. Banneker, Jean du Sable, P. Cuffee, J. Chavis, P. Salem.)†

5 DRAKE, St. Clair. "Recent Trends in Research on the Negro in the United States." *ISSB*, IX (1957), 475–92.*

6 DRAKE, St. Clair. "The Social and Economic Status of the Negro in the United States." *Daedalus*, XCIV (1965), 771–814.

7 DRAKE, St. Clair and Horace R. CAYTON. *Black Metropolis*. New York: Harper, 1945.†

8 DUBERMAN, Martin B. *In White America: A Documentary Play*. Boston: Houghton Mifflin, 1964.†

9 DUBOIS, W. E. B. *Black Folk: Then and Now*. New York: Holt, 1939.

10 DUBOIS, W. E. B. *Black Reconstruction*. New York: Russell & Russell, 1964. (Orig. pub., 1935; bibliography.)*†

11 DUBOIS, W. E. B. *The Gift of Black Folk: Negroes in the Making of America*. Boston: Stratford, 1924.*†

12 DUBOIS, W. E. B., ed. *The Negro Church*. Atlanta, Ga.: Atlanta U, 1903.

13 *Ebony* Magazine Editors, eds. *The White Problem in America*. Chicago: Johnson, 1967. (Essays by Baldwin, Killens, Lomax, King, Rowan, Clark, Young *et al.*)*

14 EDWARDS, G. Franklin. *The Negro Professional Class*. Glencoe, Ill.: Free P, 1959.

15 ELKINS, Stanley M. *Slavery: A Problem in American Institutional and Intellectual Life*. New York: Universal, 1963.†

16 EMBREE, Edwin R. *Brown Americans*. New York: Viking, 1943.

17 EMBREE, Edwin R. *Brown America: The Story of a New Race*. New York: Viking, 1931.

18 EMBREE, Edwin R. *13 Against the Odds*. Port Washington, N.Y.: Kennikat, 1967. (Biographies; orig. pub. 1944.)

19 EPPS, Archie, ed. *The Speeches of Malcolm X at Harvard*. New York: Morrow, 1968.†

20 ESSIEN-UDOM, Essien U. *Black Nationalism: A Search for an Identity in America*. Chicago: U of Chicago P, 1962.†

21 FANON, Frantz. *Black Skin, White Masks*. New York: Grove, 1967.†

22 FAUSET, Arthur H. *Black Gods of the Metropolis*. Philadelphia: U of Pennsylvania P, 1944.*

23 FISHEL, Leslie H. and Benjamin QUARLES, eds. *The American Negro: A Documentary Story*. Chicago: Scott, Foresman, 1967.*†

24 FONER, Philip S. *Frederick Douglass, a Biography*. New York: Citadel, 1964.†

25 FONER, Philip S. *Life and Writings of Frederick Douglass*. 4 vols. New York: International Pub., 1950–55.*†

1 FRANKLIN, John Hope. *The Emancipation Proclamation.* Garden City. N.Y.: Doubleday, 1963.†

2 FRANKLIN, John Hope. *From Slavery to Freedom.* 2nd ed. New York: Knopf, 1956.*†

3 FRANKLIN, John Hope. *Reconstruction after the Civil War.* Chicago: U of Chicago P, 1961.*†

4 FRAZIER, E. Franklin. *Black Bourgeoisie.* Glencoe, Ill: Free, 1962. (Orig. pub. 1957.)*†

5 FRAZIER, E. Franklin. *The Negro Church in America.* New York: Schocken, 1963.*†

6 FRAZIER, E. Franklin. *The Negro Family in the United States.* Rev. and abridged. Chicago: U of Chicago P, 1966. (Orig. pub. 1939.)*†

7 FRAZIER, E. Franklin. *The Negro in the United States.* Rev. ed. New York: Macmillan, 1957.*

8 FRAZIER, E. Franklin. *Negro Youth at the Crossways.* Washington, D.C.: American Council on Education, 1940.†

9 FURNAS, J. C. *Goodbye to Uncle Tom.* New York: Sloane, 1956.*†

10 GOLDSTON, Robert. *The Negro Revolution.* New York: Macmillan, 1968.

11 GRANT, Joanne, ed. *Black Protest: History, Documents, and Analyses 1619 to the Present.* New York: Fawcett, 1968.†

12 GREENE, Lorenzo J. *The Negro in Colonial New England, 1620–1776.* New York: Columbia UP, 1942.†

13 GRIER, William H. and Price M. COBBS. *Black Rage.* New York: Basic Books, 1968.

14 HALASZ, Nicholas. *The Rattling Chain.* New York: McKay, 1966. (Slave rebellions.)

15 HANSBERRY, Lorraine. *The Movement: Documentary of a Struggle for Equality.* New York: Simon and Schuster, 1964.†

16 "Harlem, Mecca of the New Negro." *SurG,* VI (March, 1925). (Entire issue; individual entries are listed by author in appropriate sections of this bibliography.)*

17 HAWKINS, Hugh. *Booker T. Washington and His Critics: The Problem of Negro Leadership.* Boston: Heath, 1962. (Bibliography.)†

18 HENTOFF, Nat *et al.* "The Negro in American Culture." *Cross Currents,* XI (Summer, 1961), 205–24.

19 HERNTON, Calvin C. *White Papers for White Americans.* Garden City, N.Y.: Doubleday, 1967.*

20 HERSKOVITS, Melville J. *The Myth of the Negro Past.* New York: Harper, 1964. (Orig. pub. in 1941.)*†

21 HERSKOVITS, Melville J. "Phylon Profile, X: Problem, Method, and Theory in Afro-American Studies." *Phylon,* VII (1946), 337–54.*

22 HILL, Roy L., ed. *The Rhetoric of Racial Revolt.* Denver: Golden Bell, 1964. (Speeches.)

23 HOLMES, Eugene C. "Alain Leroy Locke: A Sketch." *Phylon,* XX (1959), 82–89.*

24 HOLMES, Dwight O. W. *The Evolution of the Negro College.* New York: Teachers College, Columbia U, 1934.

1   HUGHES, Langston. *Fight for Freedom: The Story of the NAACP.* New York: Norton, 1962.

2   ISAACS, Harold. *The New World of Negro Americans.* New York: Day, 1963.†

3   JOHNSON, Charles S. *The Negro in American Civilization.* New York: Holt, 1930.*

4   JOHNSON, James Weldon. *Black Manhattan.* New York: Knopf, 1930.*†

5   JOHNSON, James Weldon. "Harlem: The Culture Capital." See 12.25, pp. 301–11.

6   JOHNSON, James Weldon. "The Making of Harlem." See 11.16, pp. 635–639.

7   JONES, Iva G. "Trollope, Carlyle, and Mill on the Negro: An Episode in the History of Ideas." *JNH,* LII (1967), 185–189.

8   JONES, LeRoi. "Black Bourgeoisie." *Harpers,* CCXXX (April, 1965), 158.

9   JONES, LeRoi. *Black Music.* New York: Morrow, 1967.†

10   JONES, LeRoi. *Blues People: Negro Music in White America.* New York: Morrow, 1963.†

11   KAISER, Ernest. See 2.1.*

12   KARON, Bertram P. *The Negro Personality: A Rigorous Investigation of the Effects of Culture.* New York: Springer, 1963.†

13   KATZ, William L., ed. *Eyewitness: The Negro in American History.* New York: Pitman, 1967.†

14   KING, Martin Luther, Jr. *Strength to Love.* New York: Harper, 1963.†

15   KING, Martin Luther, Jr. *Stride Toward Freedom: The Montgomery Story.* New York: Harper, 1958.†

16   KING, Martin Luther, Jr. *Where Do We Go From Here: Chaos or Community?* New York: Harper and Row, 1967.†

17   KING, Martin Luther, Jr. *Why We Can't Wait.* New York: Harper, 1964.*†

18   LERNER, Gerda. *The Grimké Sisters from South Carolina; Rebels against Slavery.* Boston: Houghton Mifflin, 1967.

19   LESTER, Julius. *Look Out, Whitey. Black Power's Gon' Get Your Mama!* New York: Dial, 1968.

20   LIGHTFOOT, Claude M. *Ghetto Rebellion to Black Liberation.* New York: International Pub., 1968.†

21   LINCOLN, C. Eric. *Sounds of the Struggle; Poems and Perspectives in Civil Rights.* New York: Morrow, 1967.†

22   LOCKE, Alain. "Enter the New Negro." See 11.16, pp. 631–34.

23   LOCKE, Alain. "Harlem." See 11.16, pp. 629–30.

24   LOCKE, Alain. "Negro Contribution to America." *WoT,* XII (June, 1929), 225–57.

25   LOCKE, Alain, ed. *The New Negro; an Interpretation.* New York: Boni, 1925. (Bibliography.)*

26   LOCKE, Alain. "The New Negro." See 12.25, pp. 3–18.

27   LOCKE, Alain. *When Peoples Meet.* New York: Progressive Ed. Assn., 1942.*

1 LOGAN, Rayford. *The Betrayal of the Negro*. New York: Collier, 1965. (Orig. title: *The Negro in American Life and Thought*.)*†

2 LOGAN, Rayford. *The Negro in American Life and Thought: The Nadir, 1877–1901*. New York: Dial, 1954.*

3 LOGAN, Rayford. *The Negro in the United States: A Brief Review*. Princeton, N.J.: Van Nostrand, 1957.*†

4 LOGAN, Rayford and Irving S. COHEN. *The American Negro*. Boston: Houghton Mifflin, 1967.†

5 LOMAX, Louis E. *The Negro Revolt*. New York: Harper, 1962.†

6 MARTIN, Fletcher, ed. *Our Great Americans*. Chicago: The Author, 1953.

7 MARX, Gary T. *Protest and Prejudice: A Study of Belief in the Black Community*. New York: Harper & Row, 1968.

8 MAYS, Benjamin. *The Negro's God, as Reflected in His Literature*. Boston: Grimes and Chapman, 1938. (Bibliography.)*

9 MEIER, August. *Negro Thought in America, 1880–1915: Racial Ideologies in the Age of Booker T. Washington*. Ann Arbor: U of Michigan P, 1963.*†

10 MEIER, August and F. L. BRODERICK, eds. See 8.20.

11 MEIER, August and Elliott M. RUDWICK. *From Plantation to Ghetto: An Interpretive History of American Negroes*. New York: Hill and Wang, 1966.*†

12 MELTZER, Milton. *In Their Own Words: A History of the American Negro, 1865–1916*. 3 vols. New York: Crowell, 1964–67.†

13 MILLER, Kelly. *Race Adjustment; Essays on the Negro in America*. New York: Schocken, 1968. (Orig. pub. 1908.)†

14 MOON, Bucklin. *Primer for White Folks*. Garden City, N.Y.: Doubleday, 1945.

15 MYRDAL, Gunnar. *An American Dilemma*. 2 vols. New York: Harper, 1963. (Re-issued with new preface and postscript; originally published in 1944.)*†

16 OLSEN, Otto. *Carpetbagger's Crusade: The Life of Albion W. Tourgée*. Baltimore: John Hopkins P, 1965.

17 OSOFSKY, Gilbert. *The Burden of Race; a Documentary History of Negro-White Relations in America*. New York: Harper & Row, 1967.

18 OTTLEY, Roi. *Black Odyssey*. New York: Scribner, 1948.

19 OTTLEY, Roi. *The Lonely Warrior: The Life and Times of Robert S. Abbott*. Chicago: Regnery, 1955.

20 OTTLEY, Roi. *New World a'Coming; Inside Black America*. Boston: Houghton Mifflin, 1943.

21 OTTLEY, Roi. *No Green Pastures*. New York: Scribner, 1952.

22 PARSONS, Talcott and Kenneth CLARK, eds. *The Negro American*. Boston: Houghton Mifflin, 1966.†

23 PETTIGREW, Thomas. *A Profile of the Negro American*. Princeton, N.J.: Van Nostrand, 1964.†

24 POWDERMAKER, Hortense. *After Freedom: A Cultural Study in the Deep South*. New York: Viking, 1939.†

25 PRITCHETT, Newbell Niles. *Folk Beliefs of the Southern Negro*. Chapel Hill: U of North Carolina P, 1926.

1 PROUDFOOT, Merrill. *Diary of a Sit-In.* Chapel Hill: U of North Carolina P, 1962.†

2 QUARLES, Benjamin. *The Negro in the American Revolution.* Chapel Hill: U of North Carolina P, 1961.*†

3 QUARLES, Benjamin. *The Negro in the Civil War.* Boston: Little, Brown, 1953.

4 QUARLES, Benjamin. *The Negro in the Making of America.* New York: Collier, 1964.*†

5 REDDING, Saunders. *The Lonesome Road: The Story of the Negro's Part in America.* Garden City, N.Y.: Doubleday, 1958.

6 REDDING, Saunders. *The Negro.* Washington, D.C.: Potomac Books, 1967.

7 REDDING, Saunders. *They Came in Chains.* Philadelphia: Lippincott, 1950.

8 REID, Ira De A. "The American Negro." *Understanding Minority Groups.* Ed. Joseph B. Gittler. New York: Wiley, 1956.†

9 *Report of the National Advisory Commission on Civil Disorders.* New York: Dutton, 1968.†

10 RICHARDSON, Ben. *Great American Negroes.* New York: Crowell, 1956

11 ROBINSON, Wilhelmina S. *Historical Negro Biographies.* New York: Publishers, 1967.

12 ROGERS, Joel A. *Africa's Gift to America.* Rev. ed. New York: The Author, 1961.

13 ROGERS, Joel A. *The World's Great Men of Color, 3000 B.C. to 1946 A.D.* 2 vols. New York: The Author, 1946–47.

14 ROLLINS, Charlemae H. *They Showed the Way.* New York: Crowell, 1964.

15 SCALLY, Sister Mary Anthony. See 3.2.

16 SCHUYLER, George S. "Phylon Profile, XXII: Carl Van Vechten." *Phylon,* XI (1950), 362–68.

17 SILBERMAN, Charles E. *Crisis in Black and White.* New York: Random, 1964.†

18 SLOAN, Irvin J. See 4.21.

19 SMITH, Lillian. *Killers of the Dream.* New York: Norton, 1949.†

20 STAMPP, Kenneth M. *The Peculiar Institution: Slavery in the Ante-Bellum South.* New York: Knopf, 1956.*†

21 STARKEY, Marion L. *Striving to Make It My Home: The Story of Americans from Africa.* New York: Norton, 1964. (Excellent study of African family life.)

22 STERLING, Dorothy and Benjamin QUARLES. *Lift Every Voice: The Lives of Booker T. Washington, W. E. B. DuBois, Mary Church Terrell, and James Weldon Johnson.* Garden City, N.Y.: Doubleday, 1965.†

23 STERLING, Philip and Rayford LOGAN. *Four Took Freedom: The Lives of Harriet Tubman, Frederick Douglass, Robert Smalls, and Blanche K. Bruce.* New York: Zenith, 1967.†

24 TANDY, Jeanette. "Pro-Slavery Propaganda in American Fiction of the Fifties." *SAQ,* XXII (1922), 41–50, 170–78.

25 TAYLOR, Julius H., ed. *The Negro in Science.* Baltimore: Morgan State Col. P, 1955.

1 THOMPSON, Daniel C. *The Negro Leadership Class*. Englewood Cliffs, N.J.: Prentice-Hall, 1963.†

2 THORPE, Earl E. *Negro Historians in the United States*. Baton Rouge, La.: Fraternal, 1958.

3 THORPE, Earl E. *The Mind of the Negro: An Intellectual History of Afro-Americans*. Baton Rouge, La.: Ortlieb, 1961.

4 TURNER, Arlin, ed. "Introduction." *The Negro Question: A Selection of Writings on Civil Rights in the South*. Garden City, N.Y.: Doubleday, 1958.†

5 TURNER, Darwin T. and Jean M. BRIGHT, eds *Images of the Negro in Literature*. Boston: Heath, 1965. (Essays by several Negro writers.)

6 U.S. Library of Congress. *75 Years of Freedom*. Washington, D.C.: *Government Printing Office*, 1943. (Bibliography.)

7 WARREN, Robert Penn. *Who Speaks for the Negro?* New York: Random, 1965.†

8 WASHINGTON, Booker T. *The Story of the Negro*. 2 vols. New York: Doubleday, Page, 1909.

9 WESLEY, Charles H. and Patricia W. ROMERO. *Negro Americans in the Civil War*. 2nd ed. New York: Publishers, 1968.

10 WILLIAMS, John A., ed. *The Angry Black*. New York: Lancer, 1962.

11 WILLIAMS, John A., ed. *Beyond the Angry Black*. New York: Cooper, 1966.*

12 WOODSON, Carter G. *The History of the Negro Church*. Washington, D.C.: Associated Pub., 1921.*

13 WOODSON, Carter G., ed. *Negro Orators and Their Orations*. Washington, D.C.: Associated Pub., 1925.

14 WOODSON, Carter G. *The Negro Professional Man and the Community*. Washington, D.C.: Assn for Study of Negro Life and History, 1934.*

15 WOODSON, Carter G. *The Story of the Negro Retold*. 4th ed. Washington, D.C.: Associated Pub., 1959.

16 WOODSON, Carter G. and Charles H. WESLEY. *The Negro in Our History*. 10th ed., rev. and enlarged. Washington, D.C.: Associated Pub., 1962.*

17 WOODWARD, C. Vann. *The Strange Career of Jim Crow*. 2nd rev. ed. New York: Oxford UP, 1966.†

18 WRIGHT, Nathan. *Black Power and Urban Unrest; Creative Possibilities*. New York: Hawthorn, 1967.†

19 WRIGHT, Nathan. *Ready to Riot*. New York: Holt, Rinehart and Winston, 1968.

20 WRIGHT, Richard. *Black Power: A Record of Reaction in a Land of Pathos*. New York: Harper, 1954. (Africa today.)

21 WRIGHT, Richard. *12 Million Black Voices: A Folk History of the Negro in the United States*. New York: Viking, 1941

Art, Journalism, Music, Theatre

22 BOND, Frederick W. *The Negro and the Drama: The Direct and Indirect Contribution Which the American Negro Has Made to Drama and the Legitimate Stage*. Washington, D.C.: Associated Pub., 1940.

1 BRAITHWAITE, William S. "Negro America's First Magazine." *ND*, V (Nov., 1947), 21–26.

2 BRAWLEY, Benjamin. See 21.19, 21.21.

3 BROOKS, Maxwell R. *The Negro Press Re-examined: Political Content of Leading Negro Newspapers*. Boston: Christopher, 1959.

4 BROWN, Sterling A. "The Blues." *Phylon*, XIII (1952), 286–92.

5 BROWN, Sterling A. "Negro Folk Expression: Spirituals, Seculars, Ballads, and Songs." *Phylon*, XIV (1953), 45–61.

6 BROWN, Sterling A. *The Negro on the Stage, 1937*. (Materials compiled for the Carnegie-Myrdal Study. Available on microfilm from several university libraries including California at Berkeley, Chicago, Fisk, Harvard, and North Carolina at Chapel Hill.)*

7 BUTCHER, Margaret. See 9.7.

8 CAMPBELL, Dick. "Is There a Conspiracy against Black Playwrights?" *ND*, XVII (April, 1968), 11–15.

9 CHARTERS, Samuel B. See 9.12.

10 COLERIDGE-TAYLOR, Samuel. *Twenty-Four Negro Melodies Transcribed for Piano*. New York: Ditson, 1905.

11 COURLANDER, Harold. *Negro Folk Music, U.S.A.* New York: Columbia UP, 1963.

12 CRIPPS, Thomas R. "The Death of Rastus: Negroes in American Films since 1945." *Phylon*, XXVIII (1967), 267–275.

13 CUNEY-HARE, Maud. *Negro Musicians and Their Music*. Washington, D.C.: Associated Pub., 1936.

14 DAVIS, Ossie. "The Flight from Broadway." *ND*, XV (April, 1966), 14–19.

15 DEE, Ruby. "The Tattered Queens." *ND*, XV (April, 1966), 32–36.

16 DENNISON, Tim, Sr. *The American Negro and His Amazing Music*. New York: Vintage, 1963.

17 DETWEILER, Frederick G. *The Negro Press in the United States*. Chicago: U of Chicago P, 1922.

18 DODSON, Owen. "Playwrights in Dark Glasses." *ND*, XVII (April, 1968), 30–36.*

19 DOVER, Cedric. *American Negro Art*. 3rd ed. New York: Dover, 1965.*†

20 FINKELSTEIN, Sidney. *Jazz: A People's Music*. New York: Citadel, 1948.

21 FISHER, Miles M. *Negro Slave Songs in the United States*. New York: Citadel, 1963.†

22 FLETCHER, Tom. *100 Years of the Negro in Show Business*. New York: Burdge, 1954.

23 FULLER, Hoyt W. "Black Theater in America." *ND*, XVII (April, 1968), 83–93.

24 GORE, George W. *Negro Journalism: an Essay on the History and Present Conditions of the Negro Press*. Greencastle, Ind.: Journalism, 1922.

1 GRISSOM, Mary A. *The Negro Sings a New Heaven.* Chapel Hill: U of North Carolina P, 1930.

2 HANDY, W. C. and Abbe NILES, eds. *Treasury of the Blues.* New York: Boni, 1949.

3 HENTOFF, Nat. *The Jazz Life.* New York: Dial, 1961.

4 HERNTON, Calvin C. "And You Too, Sidney Poitier!" See 11.19, pp. 53–70.

5 HOYT, Edwin P. *Paul Robeson: The American Othello.* New York: World, 1967.

6 HUGHES, Langston. *Famous Negro Music Makers.* New York: Dodd-Mead, 1955.

7 HUGHES, Langston. *First Book of Jazz.* New York: Watts, 1955.

8 HUGHES, Langston and Milton MELTZER. *Black Magic: A Pictorial History of the Negro in American Entertainment.* New York: Prentice-Hall, 1967.*

9 ISAACS, Edith R. See 30.6.

10 JACKSON, Clyde O. *The Songs of Our Years: A Study of Negro Folk Music.* New York: Exposition, 1968.

11 JEFFERSON, Miles M. "The Negro on Broadway." *Phylon,* VI (1945), 42–52; VII (1946), 185–96; VIII (1947), 146–59; IX (1948), 99–107; X (1949), 103–11; XI (1950), 105–13; XII (1951), 128–36; XIII (1952), 199–208; XIV (1953), 268–79; XV (1954), 253–60; XVII (1956), 227–37; XVIII (1957), 286–95.

12 JEROME, V. J. *The Negro in Hollywood Films.* New York: Masses and Mainstream, 1950.

13 JOHNSON, Charles S. *The Rise of the Negro Magazine.* Yellow Springs, Ohio: Antioch College P, 1948. (Bibliography.)

14 JOHNSON, James Weldon, ed. *The Book of American Negro Spirituals.* New York: Viking, 1947.*

15 JONES, LeRoi. See 12.9, 12.10.

16 KARENGA, Ron. "Black Art: A Rhythmic Reality of Revolution." *ND,* XVII (Jan., 1968.), 5–9.

17 KERLIN, Robert T. *A Decade of Negro Self-Expression.* Charlottesville, Va.: Michie, 1928. (Bibliography.)

18 KERLIN, Robert T. *The Voice of the Negro.* New York: Dutton, 1920.

19 KING, Woodie, Jr. "Problems Facing Negro Actors." *ND,* XV (April, 1966), 53–59.

20 KREBHIEL, Henry Edward. *Afro-American Folksongs: A Study in Racial and National Music.* New York: Schirmer, 1914.

21 "Krigwa Players' Little Negro Theatre." *C,* XXXIII (1926), 134–36.

22 LEWIS, C. L. "Black Knight of the Theater: Ira Aldridge." *ND,* XVII (April, 1968), 44–47.

23 LOCKE, Alain. *The Negro and His Music.* Washington, D.C.: Associates in Folk Ed., 1936.

24 LOCKE, Alain. *Negro Art: Past and Present.* Washington, D.C.: Associates in Folk Ed., 1936.

25 LOCKE, Alain. *The Negro in Art: a Pictorial Record of the Negro Artist and of the Negro Theme in Art.* Washington, D.C.: Associates in Folk Ed., 1940.

26 LOCKE, Alain. See 12.24, 12.25, 12.26.

1 LONG, Richard A. "Crisis of Consciousness." *ND*, XVII (May, 1968), 88–92.

2 MARSHALL, Herbert and Mildred STOCK. *Ira Aldridge*. New York: Macmillan, 1958.†

3 MERRIAM, Alan P. *A Bibliography of Jazz*. Philadelphia: Am. Folklore Soc., 1954.

4 MILNER, Ronald. "Black Theater—Go Home." *ND*, XVII (April, 1968), 5–10.

5 MITCHELL, Loften. *Black Drama: The Story of the American Negro in the Theater*. New York: Hawthorn, 1967.*

6 NATHAN, Hans. *Dan Emmett and the Rise of Early Negro Minstrels*. Norman: U of Oklahoma P, 1962.

7 NOBLE, Peter. *The Negro in Films*. London: Robinson, 1948.

8 OAK, Vishnu V. *The Negro Newspaper*. Yellow Springs, Ohio: Antioch, 1948. (Bibliography.)

9 ODUM, Howard Washington and Guy B. JOHNSON. *The Negro and His Songs*. Chapel Hill: U of North Carolina P, 1925.

10 ODUM, Howard Washington and Guy B. JOHNSON. *Negro Workaday Songs*. Chapel Hill: U of North Carolina P, 1926.

11 OLIVER, Paul. *Blues Fell This Morning: The Meaning of the Blues*. New York: Horizon, 1960.†

12 OLIVER, Paul. *Conversation with the Blues*. New York: Horizon, 1965.

13 O'NEAL, Frederick. "Problems and Prospects." *ND*, XV (April, 1966), 4–12. (The Negro actor.)

14 PATTERSON, Lindsay, ed. *The Negro in Music and Art*. See 4.11.

15 PENN, Irvine G. *The Afro-American Press and Its Editors*. Springfield, Mass.: Willey, 1891.

16 PORTER, James A. *Modern Negro Art*. New York: Dryden, 1960.

17 *The Portrayal of the Negro in American Painting*. Brunswick, Maine: Bowdoin College Museum of Art, 1964.

18 PRIDE, Armistead S. *A Register and History of Negro Newspapers in the United States, 1829–1950*. Evanston, Ill: Northwestern U. (Ph.D. dissertation; microfilm.)

19 SCARBOROUGH, Dorothy. *On the Trail of Negro Folk Songs*. Cambridge, Mass.: Harvard UP, 1925.

20 SHAPIRO, Nat and Nat HENTOFF, eds. *Hear Me Talkin' to Ya: The Story of Jazz by the Men Who Made It*. New York: Rinehart, 1955.†

21 STEARNS, Marshall W. *The Story of Jazz*. New York: Mentor, 1958.†

22 TERKEL, Louis (Studs). *Giants of Jazz*. New York: Crowell, 1957.

23 THURMAN, Howard. *Deep River*. New York: Harper, 1955.

24 ULANOV, Barry. *A Handbook of Jazz*. New York: Viking, 1957.†

25 ULANOV, Barry. *A History of Jazz in America*. New York: Viking, 1952.

Literary History and Criticism

Anthologies

1 ADOFF, Arnold, ed. *I am the Darker Brother; an Anthology of Modern Poems by Negro Americans.* New York: Macmillan, 1968.

2 ALHAMISI, Ahmed and Harun K. WANGARA, eds. *Black Arts: Anthology of Black Creations.* Detroit: Broadside, 1970.

3 BONTEMPS, Arna, ed. *American Negro Poetry.* New York: Hill and Wang, 1963.*†

4 BONTEMPS, Arna, ed. *Golden Slippers: An Anthology of Poetry for Young Readers.* New York: Harper, 1941.

5 BRAWLEY, Benjamin, ed. *Early Negro American Writers; Selections with Bibliographical and Critical Introduction.* Chapel Hill: U of North Carolina P, 1935. (Bibliography.)*

6 BREMAN, Paul, ed. *Sixes and Sevens: An Anthology of New Negro Poetry.* London: Breman, 1962.†

7 BREWER, J. Mason, ed. *Heralding Dawn: An Anthology of Verse.* Dallas, Texas: Thomason, 1936.

8 BROWN, Sterling A., ed. *American Stuff.* New York: Viking, 1937.

9 BROWN, Sterling A., Arthur DAVIS, and Ulysses LEE, eds. *The Negro Caravan.* New York: Dryden, 1941. (Bibliography and biographical materials.)*

10 CALVERTON, Victor F., ed. *An Anthology of American Negro Literature.* New York: Random, 1929. [Modern Lib.]

11 CHAPMAN, Abraham, ed. *Black Voices.* New York: Dell, 1968.*†

12 CLARKE, John Henrik, ed. *American Negro Short Stories.* New York: Hill and Wang, 1967.

13 CROMWELL, Otelia, Lorenzo D. TURNER, and Eva B. DYKES, eds. *Readings from Negro Authors.* New York: Harcourt, Brace, 1931.

14 COUCH, William, ed. *Black Playwrights; an Anthology.* Baton Rouge, La., Louisiana State UP, 1968.

15 CULLEN, Countee, ed. *Caroling Dusk; an Anthology of Verse by Negro Poets.* New York: Harper, 1927.

16 CUNARD, Nancy, ed. *Negro Anthology.* London: Wishart, 1934.

17 DREER, Herman, ed. *American Literature by Negro Authors.* New York: Macmillan, 1950. (Bibliography.)

18 EMANUEL, James A., and Theodore GROSS, eds. *Dark Symphony: Negro Literature in America.* New York: Free P, 1968. (Bibliography.)*†

19 FORD, Nick Aaron and H. L. FAGGETT, eds. *Best Short Stories by Afro-American Writers, 1925–1950.* Boston: Meador, 1950.

20 HAYDEN, Robert, ed. *Kaleidoscope, Poems by American Negro Poets.* New York: Harcourt, Brace & World, 1967.

1 HILL, Herbert, ed. *Soon, One Morning: New Writings by American Negroes, 1940–1962.* New York: Knopf, 1963.*

2 HUGHES, Langston, ed. *The Best Short Stories by Negro Writers: An Anthology from 1899 to the Present.* Boston and Toronto: Little, Brown, 1967.*†

3 HUGHES, Langston, ed. *La poésie negro-américaine.* Paris: Seghers, 1966.

4 HUGHES, Langston, ed. *Negro Poets U.S.A.* Bloomington: Indiana UP, 1964.

5 HUGHES, Langston and Arna BONTEMPS, eds. *The Poetry of the Negro, 1746–1949.* Garden City, N.Y.: Doubleday, 1949. (Biographical materials.)*

6 JOHNSON, Charles S., ed. *Ebony and Topaz: A Collectanea.* New York: National Urban League, 1927.*

7 JOHNSON, James W., ed. *The Book of American Negro Poetry.* Rev. ed. New York: Harcourt, Brace, 1931. (Bibliography.)*

8 JOHNSON, James W. See 17.14.

9 JONES, LeRoi and Larry NEAL, eds. *Black Fire.* New York: Morrow, 1968.

10 KERLIN, Robert T., ed. *Contemporary Poetry of the Negro.* Hampton, Va.: Hampton Institute P, 1923. (Bibliography.)

11 KERLIN, Robert T., ed. *Negro Poets and Their Poems.* 2nd ed. Washington: Associated Pub., 1935.

12 LANUSSE, Armand, ed. *Creole Voices: Poems in French by Free Men of Color.* Centennial ed. Washington, D.C.: Associated Pub., 1945. (Orig. pub. in 1845.)

13 LOCKE, Alain. See 12.25.

14 LOCKE, Alain, ed. *Four Negro Poets.* New York: Simon and Schuster, 1927. (Works of Claude McKay, Countee Cullen, Jean Toomer, and Langston Hughes, with critical commentaries by the editor.)*

15 LOCKE, Alain and Montgomery GREGORY, eds. *Plays of Negro Life: A Source-Book of Native American Drama.* New York: Harper, 1927.

16 MARCUS, Shmuel, ed. *Anthology of Revolutionary Poetry.* New York: Active, 1929.

17 MURPHY, Beatrice, ed. *Ebony Rhythm.* New York: Exposition, 1948.

18 MURPHY, Beatrice, ed. *Negro Voices; an Anthology of Contemporary Verse.* New York: Harrison, 1938.

19 PEREZ ECHAVARRIA, Miguel Ramon, ed. *La poesía negra en America.* Buenos Aires: Nocito & Rano, 1946.

20 PERKINS, Eugene, ed. *Black Expressions: An Anthology of New Black Poets.* Chicago: Conda, 1967.

21 POOL, Rosey E., ed. *Beyond the Blues: New Poems by American Negroes.* Lympne, Kent, England: Hand and Flower, 1962.*†

22 POOL, Rosey E., ed. *Black and Unknown Bards.* Aldington, Kent, England: Hand and Flower, 1958.

23 RICHARDSON, Willis, ed. *Plays and Pageants from the Life of the Negro.* Washington, D.C.: Associated Pub., 1930. (Bibliography.)*

24 RICHARDSON, Willis and May MILLER, eds. *Negro History in Thirteen Plays.* Washington, D.C.: Associated Pub., 1935.

25 SHUMAN, R. Baird, ed. *Nine Black Poets.* Durham, N.C.: Moore, 1968.

1 *Ten: Anthology of Detroit Poets*. Fort Smith, Ark.: South and West, 1968.

2 TURNER, Darwin T., ed. *Black American Literature: Essays*. Columbus, Ohio: Merrill, 1969.*†

3 TURNER, Darwin T., ed. *Black American Literature: Fiction*. Columbus, Ohio: Merrill, 1969.*†

4 TURNER, Darwin T., ed. *Black American Literature: Poetry*. Columbus, Ohio: Merrill, 1969.*†

5 WATKINS, Sylvester C., ed. *Anthology of American Negro Literature*. New York: Random, 1944. [Modern Lib.]

6 WHITE, Newman and W. C. JACKSON, eds. *An Anthology of Verse by American Negroes*. Durham, N.C.: Moore, 1968. [Originally pub., 1924.]

7 WILLIAMS, John A., ed. See 15.10, 15.11.

General History and Criticism

This section includes books and articles concerned with more than one genre.

8 ADAMS, Agatha. *Contemporary Negro Arts*. Chapel Hill: U of North Carolina P, 1948.

9 ALLEN, Samuel. "Negritude and Its Relevance to the American Negro Writer." See 21.10, pp. 8–20.

10 *The American Negro Writer and His Roots*. New York: American Society of African Culture, 1960. (Collection of essays from first Conference of Negro Writers.)*

11 BLUE, Ila J. *A Study of Literary Criticism by Some Negro Writers, 1900–1955*. Ann Arbor: U of Michigan, 1960. (Unpublished dissertation.)*

12 BONTEMPS, Arna. "Famous WPA Authors." *ND*, VIII (June, 1950), 43–47.

13 BONTEMPS, Arna. "The Harlem Renaissance." *SatR*, XXX (March 22, 1947), 12–13, 44.

14 BONTEMPS, Arna. "The Negro Contribution to American Letters." See 4.5, pp. 850–78.

15 BRAITHWAITE, William S. "Alain Locke's Relationship to the Negro in American Literature." *Phylon*, XVIII (1957), 166–73.*

16 BRAITHWAITE, William S. "The Negro in American Literature." See 12.25.*

17 BRAITHWAITE, William S. "The Negro in Literature." *C*, XXVIII (1924), 204–10.

18 BRAWLEY, Benjamin. See 19.5.

19 BRAWLEY, Benjamin. *The Negro Genius*. New York: Dodd, Mead, 1937.* (Bibliography.)

20 BRAWLEY, Benjamin. "The Negro in American Literature." *Bookman*, LVI (October, 1922), 137–41. (Bibliography.)

21 BRAWLEY, Benjamin. *The Negro in Literature and Art*. 3rd ed. New York: Dodd, Mead, 1929.*

1 BRAWLEY, Benjamin. "The Negro Literary Renaissance." *SoW*, LVI (1927), 177–80.

2 BRAWLEY, Benjamin. "The Promise of Negro Literature." *JNH*, XIX (1934), 53–59.

3 BREWSTER, Dorothy. "From Phillis Wheatley to Richard Wright." *NQ*, I (1945), 80–83.

4 BROOKS, Russell. "The Comic Spirit and the Negro's New Look." *CLAJ*, VI (1962), 35–43.

5 BROWN, Lloyd. "Which Way for the Negro Writer?" *M&M*, IV (March, 1951), 53–59; (April, 1951), 50–59.

6 BROWN, Sterling A. "The Negro Author and His Publisher." *NQ*, I (1945), 7–20.

7 BROWN, Sterling A., Arthur P. DAVIS and Ulysses LEE, eds. See 19.9.

8 BUTCHER, Margaret. See 9.7.

9 BUTCHER, Philip. "In Print: Our Raceless Writers." *O*, XXVI (1948), 113–14.*

10 CALVERTON, V. F. "The Advance of Negro Literature." *Opportunity*, IV (1926), 54–55.

11 CALVERTON, V. F. "Introduction." See 19.10.

12 CALVERTON, V. F. *The Liberation of American Literature.* New York: Scribner, 1932.

13 CALVERTON, V. F. "The Negro and American Culture." *SatR*, XXII (September 21, 1940), 3–4.

14 CARTEY, Wilfred. "The Realities of Four Negro Writers." *CUF*, IX, iii (1966), 34–42. (E. Mphahele, G. Lamming, C. M. de Jesus, J. Baldwin. Only Baldwin is American.)*

15 CAYTON, Horace R. "Ideological Forces in the Work of Negro Writers." See 24.14, pp. 37–50.*

16 *Carolina*, LVII (May, 1927). (Entire issue.) (Individual entries are listed by author in appropriate sections of this bibliography.)

17 *Carolina*, LVIII (May, 1928). (Entire issue.)

18 CHANDLER, G. Lewis. "A Major Problem of Negro Authors in their March towards Belles-Lettres." See 27.19, pp. 383–86.

19 CHAPMAN, Abraham. "The Harlem Renaissance in Literary History." *CLAJ*, XI (1967), 38–58.

20 CHESNUTT, Charles W. "Post-bellum, Pre-Harlem." *C*, XXXVIII (1931), 193–94.

21 CLARKE, John Henrik. "The Origin and Growth of Afro-American Literature." *ND*, XVII (Dec., 1967), 54–67.

22 CULLEN, Countee. "The Dark Tower." *O*, IV (1926), 388–90; V (1927), 24–25, 53–54, 86–87, 118–19, 149–50, 180–81, 210–11, 240–41, 272–73, 336–37; VI (1928), 51–52, 90, 120, 146–47, 178–79, 210, 271–73. (A monthly column on books and writers.)

23 DAVIS, Arthur P. "Integration and Race Literature." *Phylon* XVII (1956), 141–46.

24 DAVIS, Ossie. "The Wonderful World of Law and Order." See 24.14, pp. 154–80.*

1 DE ARMOND, Fred. "A Note on the Sociology of Negro Literature." *O*, III (1925), 369–71.

2 DOVER, Cedric. "Notes on Coloured Writing." *Phylon*, VIII (1947), 213–24.

3 DUBOIS, W. E. B. See 10.9, 10.11.

4 DUBOIS, W. E. B. "Postscript." *C*, 1910–1934. (A monthly column on literature and life from Vol. I through Vol. XLII.)

5 DUBOIS, W. E. B. "The Donor of the DuBois Literary Prize." *C*, XXXIX (1931), 157.

6 DUBOIS, W. E. B. "The DuBois Literary Prize." *C*, XXXIX (1931), 117.

7 DUBOIS, W. E. B. "The Negro in Literature and Art." *AAAP&SS*, XLIX (1913), 233–37.

8 DUBOIS, W. E. B. and Alain LOCKE. "The Younger Literary Movement." *C*, XXVII (1924), 161–63.

9 ELEAZER, Robert Burns. *Singers in the Dawn*. Atlanta, Ga.: Conference on Education and Race Relations, 1939.

10 "Ebony Book Shelf." *Ebony Magazine*. (Monthly feature—book reviews.)

11 ELLISON, Ralph. "The Negro Writer in America." *PR*, XXII (1955), 212–22.*

12 ELLISON, Ralph and Stanley Edgar HYMAN. "The Negro Writer in America." *PR*, XXV (1958), 197–211, 212–22. (Hyman, "The Folk Tradition," 197–211; Ellison, "Change the Joke and Slip the Yoke," 212–22.)

13 FERGUSON, Blanche E. *Countee Cullen and the Harlem Renaissance*. New York: Dodd, Mead, 1966.

14 FONTAINE, William T. "Toward a Philosophy of the American Negro Literature." *PA*, English ed., Nos. 24–25 (February–May, 1959), 164–76.

15 FORD, Nick Aaron. "Battle of the Books: A Critical Survey of Significant Books by and about Negroes Published in 1960." *Phylon*, XXII (1961), 119–24.

16 FORD, Nick Aaron. "A Blueprint for Negro Authors." See 27.19, pp. 374–77.

17 FORD, Nick Aaron. "The Fire Next Time? A Critical Survey of Belles Lettres by and about Negroes Published in 1963." *Phylon*, XXV (1964), 123–34.

18 FORD, Nick Aaron. "Search for Identity: A Critical Survey of Significant Belles Lettres by and about Negroes Published in 1961." *Phylon*, XXIII (1962), 128–38.

19 FORD, Nick Aaron. "Walls Do a Prison Make: A Critical Survey of Significant Belles Lettres by and about Negroes Published in 1962." *Phylon*, XXIV (1963), 123–34.

20 FORD, Thomas. "Howells and the American Negro." *TSLL*, V (1964), 530–37.

21 FULLER, Hoyt W. "The Negro Writer in the United States." *Ebony*, XX (November, 1964), 126–34.

22 FULLER, Hoyt W. "Reverberations from a Writer's Conference." *A Forum*, I, iv (1966), 11–20.

23 FULLER, Hoyt W., ed. "A Survey: Black Writers' Views on Literary Lions and Values." *ND*, XVII (Jan., 1968), 10–48, 81–89. (Includes statements by Redding, Mayfield, Margaret Walker, Gwendolyn Brooks, Killens, Hayden, "Paul Vesey" (Samuel Allen), and others.)*

1 GALE, Zona. "The Negro Sees Himself." *Survey*, LIV (1925), 300–01.

2 GILDER, Van. "Afro-American Literature." *Sch*, XXV (January 19, 1935), 9.

3 GLICKSBERG, Charles I. "The Alienation of Negro Literature." *Phylon*, XI (1950), 49–58.

4 GLICKSBERG, Charles I. "For Negro Literature: The Catharsis of Laughter." *Forum*, CVII (1947), 450–56.

5 GLICKSBERG, Charles I. "Race and Revolution in Negro Literature." *Forum*, CVIII (1947), 300–308.

6 GLICKSBERG, Charles I. "The Symbolism of Vision." *SWR*, XXXIX (1954), 259–65.

7 GLOSTER, Hugh M. "The Negro Writer and the Southern Scene." *SouP*, IV (1948), 1–3.

8 GLOSTER, Hugh M. "Race and the Negro Writer." See 27.19, pp. 369–71.

9 GORDON, Eugene. "Social and Political Problems of Negro Writers." *American Writers Congress*. New York, 1935, pp. 145–53.

10 GROSS, Seymour L. "Stereotype to Archetype: The Negro in American Literary Criticism." See 1.13.*

11 GROSS, Seymour L. and John HARDY. See 1.13.

12 "Harlem, Mecca of the New Negro." See 11.16.

13 HENTOFF, Nat. "The Other Side of the Blues." See 24.14, pp. 37–50.

14 HILL, Herbert, ed. *Anger and Beyond: The Negro Writer in the United States.* New York: Harper & Row, 1966.*†

15 HILL, Herbert. "The New Directions of the Negro Writer." *C*, LXX (1963), 205–10.

16 HILL, Leslie P. "Foreword." *The Wings of Oppression*. Boston: Stratford, 1922.

17 HOLMES, Eugene C. "Problems Facing the Negro Writer Today." *New Challenge*, I (1937), 69–75.

18 HOWARD, R. "Some Poets in Their Prose." *Phylon*, CV (1965), 403.

19 HUGHES, Langston. "Black Renaissance." See 6.17.

20 HUGHES, Langston. "Harlem Literati in the Twenties." *SatR*, XX (June 22, 1940), 12–14.*

21 HUGHES, Langston. "The Negro Artist and the Racial Mountain." *Nation*, CXXII (1926), 692–94.

22 HUGHES, Langston. "To Negro Writers." *American Writers Congress*. New York, 1935, pp. 139–47.

23 HUGHES, Langston. "The Twenties: Harlem and Its Negritude." *A Forum*, I, iv (1966), 11–20.

24 HUGHES, Langston, LeRoi JONES and John A. WILLIAMS. "Problems of the Negro Writer." *SatR*, XLVI (April 20, 1963), 19–21, 40.

25 HURSTON, Zora Neale. "What White Publishers Won't Print." *ND*, V (April, 1947), 85–89.

26 ISAACS, Harold R. "Five Writers and Their African Ancestors: Part I." *Phylon*, XXI (1960), 243–65. (L. Hughes and R. Wright.)

27 ISAACS, Harold R. "Five Writers and Their African Ancestors: Part II." *Phylon*, XXI (1960), 317–36. (Baldwin, Ellison, Hansberry.)

1 JACKSON, August V. "The Renascence of Negro Literature 1922 to 1929." Atlanta, Georgia: Atlanta University, 1936. (Master's thesis.)

2 JACKSON, Blyden. "The Blithe Newcomers: A Résumé of Negro Literature in 1954." *Phylon*, XVI (1955), 5–12.

3 JACKSON, Blyden. "The Case for American Negro Literature." *MAQR*, LXI (1955), 161–66.

4 JACKSON, Blyden. "The Continuing Strain: A Résumé of Negro Literature in 1955." *Phylon*, XVII (1956), 35–40.

5 JACKSON, Blyden. "An Essay in Criticism." See 27.19, pp. 338–43.

6 JACKSON, Blyden. "Faith without Works in Negro Literature." *Phylon*, XII (1951), 378–88.

7 JACKSON, Blyden. "Full Circle." *Phylon*, IX (1948), 30–35.

8 JACKSON, Esther M. "The American Negro and the Image of the Absurd." *Phylon*, XXIII (1962), 359–71.*

9 JACKSON, Miles M. "Significant Belles Lettres by and about Negroes Published in 1964." *Phylon*, XXVI (1965), 216–27.

10 JACOBS, George W. "Negro Authors Must Eat." *Nation*, CXXVIII (1929), 710–11.

11 JOHNSON, Charles S. "The Negro Enters Literature." See 22.16, pp. 3–9, 44–48. (Bibliography.)

12 JOHNSON, James W. See 12.4.

13 JOHNSON, James W. "The Dilemma of the Negro Author." *AMer*, XV (1928), 477–81.

14 JOHNSON, James W. "Negro Authors and White Publishers." *C*, XXXVI (1929), 313–17.

15 JOHNSON, James W. "Race Prejudice and the Negro Artist." *Harpers* CLVII (1928), 769–76.

16 JONES, LeRoi. "The Myth of a Negro Literature." *SatR*, XLVI (April 20, 1963), 20–21.

17 JONES, LeRoi. "Philistinism and the Negro Writer." See 24.14, pp. 51–61.

18 KAISER, Ernest. "The Literature of Harlem." *Freedomways*, III (1963), 276–91.*

19 KAISER, Ernest. "The Literature of Negro Revolt." *Freedomways*, III (1963), 36–47.

20 KAISER, Ernest. "Recent Books." *Freedomways*. (A long, annotated bibliography published in each issue.)

21 KERLIN, Robert T. *A Decade of Negro Self-Expression.* Charlottesville, Va.: Michie, 1928. (Bibliography.)

22 KERLIN, Robert T. *The Voice of the Negro.* New York: Dutton, 1920.

23 KESSLER, Sidney H. "Collectors, Scholars, and Negro Literature." *MJ*, VII (1954), 222–34.

24 LASH, John. "The Anthologist and the Negro Author." *Phylon*, VIII (1947), 68–76.

25 LASH, John. "The Conditioning of Servitude: A Critical Summary of Literature by and about Negroes in 1957." *Phylon*, XIX (1958), 143–54, 247–57.

26 LASH, John. "Dimension in Racial Experience: A Critical Summary of Literature by and about Negroes in 1958." *Phylon*, XX (1959), 115–31.

1   LASH, John. "Expostulation and Reply: A Critical Summary of Literature by and about Negroes in 1959." *Phylon*, XXI (1960), 111–23.

2   LASH, John. "A Long, Hard Look at the Ghetto: A Critical Summary of Literature by and about Negroes in 1956." *Phylon*, XVIII (1957), 7–24.

3   LASH, John. "On Negro Literature." *Phylon*, VI (1945), 240–47.

4   LASH, John. "The Race Consciousness of the American Negro Author." *SocF*, XXVIII (October, 1949), 24–34.

5   LASH, John. "The Study of Negro Literary Expression." *NHB*, IX (1946), 207–11.

6   LASH, John. "What Is 'Negro Literature'?" *CE*, IX (1947), 37–42.*

7   LEE, Ulysses. "Criticism at Mid-Century." See 27.19.*

8   LITTLEJOHN, David. *Black on White; a Critical Survey of Writing by American Negroes*. New York: Grossman, 1966. (Inferior judgments.)

9   LOCKE, Alain. See 12.22, 12.24, 12.25, 12.26.

10   LOCKE, Alain. "American Literary Tradition and the Negro." *ModQ*, III (1926), 215–22.

11   LOCKE, Alain. "Black Truth and Black Beauty." *O*, XI (1933), 14–18.

12   LOCKE, Alain. "A Critical Retrospect of the Literature of the Negro for 1947." *Phylon*, IX (1948), 3–12.

13   LOCKE, Alain. "Dawn Patrol: A Review of the Literature of the Negro for 1948." *Phylon*, X (1949), 5–13; Part II, 167–72.

14   LOCKE, Alain. "Deep River, Deeper Sea.... A Retrospective Review of the Literature of the Negro for 1953." *O*, XIV (1936), 6–10; Part II, 42–43, 61.

15   LOCKE, Alain. "Dry Fields and Green Pastures." *O*, XVIII (1940), 4–10, 28; Part II, 41–46, 53.

16   LOCKE, Alain. "The Eleventh Hour with Nordicism: Retrospective Review of the Literature of the Negro for 1934." *O*, XIII (1935), 8–12; Part II, 46–48, 59.

17   LOCKE, Alain. "From *Native Son* to *Invisible Man*: A Review of the Literature of the Negro for 1952." *Phylon*, XIV (1953), 34–44.

18   LOCKE, Alain. "God Save Reality! Retrospective Review of the Literature of the Negro: 1936." *O*, XV (1937), 8–13; Part II, 40–44.

19   LOCKE, Alain. "The High Price of Integration: A Review of the Literature of the Negro for 1951." *Phylon*, XIII (1952), 7–18.

20   LOCKE, Alain. "Inventory at Mid-Century: A Review of the Literature of the Negro for 1950." *Phylon*, XII (1951), 5–12.

21   LOCKE, Alain. "Jingo, Counter-Jingo and Us—Retrospective Review of the Literature of the Negro: 1937." *O*, XVI (1938), 7–11, 27; Part II, 39–42.

22   LOCKE, Alain. "The Negro in American Literature." *New World Writing No. 1*. New York: Mentor, 1952, pp. 18–33.†

23   LOCKE, Alain. "The Negro Minority in American Literature." *EJ*, XXXV (1946), 315–19.

24   LOCKE, Alain. "The Negro: 'New' or Newer." *O*, XVII (1939), 4–10; Part II, 36–42.

25   LOCKE, Alain. "The Negro's Contribution to American Art and Literature." *AAAP&SS*, CXL (1928), 234–47.

1 LOCKE, Alain. "1928: A Retrospective Review." *O*, VII (1929), 8–11.

2 LOCKE, Alain. "Of Native Sons: Real and Otherwise." *O*, XIX (1941), 4–9; Part II, 48–52.

3 LOCKE, Alain. "The Saving Grace of Realism—Retrospective Review of the Negro Literature of 1933." *O*, XII (1934), 8–11, 30.

4 LOCKE, Alain. "Self-Criticism: The Third Dimension in Culture." See 27.19, pp. 391–94.

5 LOCKE, Alain. "This Year of Grace." *O*, IX (1931), 48–51.

6 LOCKE, Alain. "Who and What is 'Negro'? A Retrospective Review of the Literature of the Negro for 1941." *O*, XX (1942), 36–41; Part II, 83–87.

7 LOCKE, Alain. "Wisdom *de Profundis:* The Literature of the Negro, 1949." See 27.19, pp. 5–14.

8 LOGGINS, Vernon. *The Negro Author, His Development in America to 1900.* New York: Columbia UP, 1931. (Reprinted by Kennikat Press, 1964. Bibliography.)*

9 MARCUS, Steven. "The American Negro in Search of Identity." *Commentary*, XVI (1953), 456–63. (Baldwin, Ellison, Hughes, Wright.)

10 MARGOLIES, Edward. *Native Sons: A Critical Study of Twentieth Century Negro American Authors.* Philadelphia: Lippincott, 1968.

11 MASON, Julian D. *The Critical Reception of American Negro Authors in American Magazines, 1800–1885.* Ann Arbor: U Microfilms, 1963. (Unpublished dissertation.)*

12 MAUND, Alfred. "The Negro Novelist and the Contemporary American Scene." *CJF*, XII (1954), 28–34.

13 MAYFIELD, Julian. "Into the Mainstream and Oblivion." See 21.10, pp. 29–33.

14 MC DONNELL, Thomas. "The Emergence of the Negro in Literature." *Critic*, XX (December, 1961–January, 1962), 31–34.

15 MILLER, Arthur, Langston HUGHES and Bruce CARLTON. "The Writer in America." *Mainstream*, X (July, 1957), 42–57.

16 MITCHELL, Loften. "The Negro Writer and His Materials." See 21.10, pp. 55–60.

17 MORRIS, Lloyd. "The Negro 'Renaissance'." *SW*, LIX (1930), 82–86.

18 MORSE, George C. "The Fictitious Negro." *Outlook and Independent*, CLII (1929), 648–49, 678–79.

19 "The Negro in Literature: The Current Scene." *Phylon*, XI (1950), 297–374. (Entire issue devoted to articles about Negro writers; individual entries are listed by author in appropriate sections of this bibliography.)*

20 NICHOLS, Charles A., Jr. "The Forties: A Decade of Growth." See 27.19, pp. 377–379.

21 NICHOLS, Charles A., Jr. "Slave Narratives and the Plantation Legend." *Phylon*, X (1949), 201–09.

22 NICHOLS, Charles A., Jr. "Who Read the Slave Narratives?" *Phylon*, XX (1949), 149–162.

23 OSOFSKY, Gilbert. "Symbols of the Jazz Age: The New Negro and Harlem Discovered." *AQ*, XVII (1965), 229–36. (Images of Negroes and Harlem in the Twenties.)

1 *Palms*, I (October, 1926). (Entire issue.)

2 PARKER, John W. "Phylon Profile, XIX: Benjamin Brawley—Teacher and Scholar." *Phylon*, X (1949), 15–24.

3 "Perspectives." *ND*. (Monthly column of notes on books, writers, artists, and the arts.)

4 RECORD, C. Wilson. "The Negro as Creative Artist." *C*, LXXII (1965), 153–58.

5 REDDING, Saunders. "American Negro Literature." *AmS*, XVIII (April, 1949), 137–48.

6 REDDING, Saunders. "The Negro Author: His Publisher, His Public, and His Purse." *PubW*, CXLVII (1945), 1284–88.

7 REDDING, Saunders. "The Negro Writer and American Literature." See 24.14, pp. 62–75.*

8 REDDING, Saunders. "The Negro Writer and His Relationship to His Roots." See 21.10, pp. 1–8.

9 REDDING, Saunders. "The Negro Writer—Shadow and Substance." See 27.19, pp. 371–373.

10 REDDING, Saunders. "Negro Writing in America." *NeL*, XLII (May 16, 1960), 8–10.

11 REDDING, Saunders. "The Problems of the Negro Writer." *MR*, VI (1964), 57–70.

12 REDDING, Saunders. "Since Richard Wright." *A Forum*, I, iv (1966), 21–31.

13 REDDING, Saunders. *To Make a Poet Black*. Chapel Hill: U of North Carolina P, 1939.*

14 REID, Ira De A. "The Literature of the Negro: A Social Scientist's Appraisal." See 27.19, pp. 388–90.

15 ROURKE, Constance. "Tradition for a Negro Literature." *Roots of American Culture*. New York: Harcourt, Brace, 1942.

16 ROUSSÈVE, Charles B. *The Negro in Louisiana: Aspects of His History and His Literature*. New Orleans: Xavier UP, 1927.

17 SCALLY, Sister May Anthony. See 3.2.

18 SCHUYLER, George S. "The Negro Art Hokum." *Nation*, CXXII (1926), 662–63.

19 SCHUYLER, George S. "The Van Vechten Revolution." See 27.19, pp. 362–68.

20 SHAPIRO, Karl. "The Decolonization of American Literature." *WLB*, XXXIX (1965), 842–53.

21 SHIH, Hsien-yung. "Impressions of American Negro Literature." *ChiR* No. 4 (1966), 107–12.

22 SMITH, William Gardner. "The Negro Writer: Pitfalls and Compensations." See 27.19, pp. 297–303.

23 SPINGARN, Arthur B. "Books by Negro Authors. . . ." *C*, XLV (1938), 47–48, 50; *C*, XLVI (1939), 45–46, 62; XLVII (1940), 46, 50; XLVIII (1941), 76–77, 89; XLIX (1942), 114–15, 142; L (1943), 45–46, 61; LII (1945), 49–50; LIII (1946), 46–47, 59–60; LIV (1947), 45–46, 60; LV (1948), 47; LVI (1949), 45–46, 62; LVII (1950), 96; LVIII (1951), 80–84; LX (1953), 83–87; LXI (1954), 84–90; LXII (1955), 83–90; LXIII (1956), 86–93; LXIV (1957), 76–82; LXV (1958), 81–86; LXVI (1959), 83–89; LXVII (1960), 237–44; LXVIII (1961), 75–81; LXIX (1962), 83–89; LXX (1963), 82–91; LXXI (1964), 82–91; LXXII (1965), 103–13.

24 SWADOS, Harvey. "The Writer in Contemporary American Society."

1   THOMPSON, Era Bell. "Negro Publications and the Writer." See 27.19, pp. 304–5.

2   THORNHILL, G. C. "Negro Becomes Literary Contributor." *Poet Lore*, XXXIX (1928), 431–35.

3   THURMAN, Wallace. "Negro Artists and the Negro." *NR*, LII (1927), 37–39.*

4   THURMAN, Wallace. "Nephews of Uncle Remus." *Independent*, CXIX (1927), 296–8.*

5   TILLMAN, Nathaniel P. "The Threshold of Maturity." See 27.19, pp. 387–88.

6   TURNER, Lorenzo. "Anti-Slavery Sentiment in American Literature Prior to 1865." *JNH*, XIV (1929), 371–492.

7   VAN DOREN, Carl. "The Roving Critic." *Century*, CXI (1926), 637–9. (The Harlem Renaissance.)

8   WETHERILL, Julie K. "The Negro as Producer of Literature." *Chautauquan*, XV (1892), 224–25.

9   WHICHER, George F. "The Resurgent South." *The Literature of the American People*. Ed. A. H. Quinn. New York: Appleton-Century-Crofts, 1951.

10 WHITE, Walter. "Negro Literature." *American Writers on American Literature*. Ed. John Macy. New York: Liveright, 1931, pp. 442–51.

11 WILLIAMS, John A. "Negro Literature Today." *Ebony*, XVIII (1963), 73–76.

12 WOOLRIDGE, Nancy. "English Critics and the Negro Writers." *Phylon*, XV (1954), 139–46.

13 WRIGHT, Richard. "Blueprint for Negro Writing." *New Challenge*, I (1937), 53–65.

14 VILLARD, O. G. "Negro Literature." *LitR*, III (1923), 797–8.

Drama

In an earlier section, entries were concerned with Afro-Americans as actors and entertainers in the theatre. Here, the emphasis is placed upon them as authors. Because relatively few Afro-Americans have produced dramas that have become widely known in the American professional theatre, most historians and critics—especially writers of books—go beyond the dramatist in order to expand the subject of their discussion. Hence, most of the important references in a study of Afro-American dramatists also include discussions of Afro-Americans as subjects of drama or as actors.

15 ALEXANDER, Lewis M. "Plays of Negro Life, A Survey." See 29.23, pp. 45–57.

16 BALDWIN, James. "Theatre: The Negro in and out." *ND*, XV (April, 1966), 37–44.

17 "Beginnings of a Negro Drama." *LitD*, XLVIII (1914), 1114.

18 BOND, Frederick W. See 15.22.

19 BRADLEY, Gerald. "Goodbye Mr. Bones: The Emergence of Negro Themes and Character in American Drama." *Drama Cr*, VII (1964), 79–86.

20 BROWN, Sterling A. See 16.6.

21 BROWN, Sterling A. *Negro Poetry and Drama*. Washington, D.C.: Associates in Negro Folk Education, 1937. (Bibliography.)*

22 BULLINS, Ed. "Theatre of Reality." *ND*, XV (April, 1966), 60–66.

23 *Carolina* LIX (April, 1929). (Entire issue.)

1 CHILDRESS, Alice. "A Woman Playwright Speaks Her Mind." *Freedomways*, VI (1966), 75–80.

2 EDMONDS, Randolph. "Some Reflections on the Negro in American Drama." *O*, VIII (1930), 303–5.

3 GRANT, G. C. "The Negro in Dramatic Art." *JNH*, XVII (1932), 19–29.

4 GREGORY, Montgomery. "The Drama of Negro Life." See 12.25, pp. 153–60.

5 HUGHES, Langston. See 17.8.

6 ISAACS, Edith R. *The Negro in the American Theatre*. New York: Theatre Arts, 1947. (Pub. orig. in *ThA*, XXVI (1942), 492–543.)

7 JOHNSON, James W. See 12.4.

8 KILLENS, John O. "Broadway in Black and White." *A Forum*, I, iii (1965), 66–70.*

9 LAWSON, Hilda J. See 2.6.

10 LOCKE, Alain. "The Drama of Negro Life." *ThA*, X (1926), 701–6.

11 MITCHELL, Loften. See 18.5.

12 MITCHELL, Loften. "The Negro Theatre and the Harlem Community." *Freedomways*, III (1963), 384–94.

13 NATHAN, H. See 18.6.

14 NEAL, Larry. "The Black Arts Movement." *TDR*, XII (Summer, 1968), 29–39.

15 PATTERSON, Lindsay, ed. *Anthology of the American Negro in the Theater*. See 4.11.

16 SHELBY, Gertrude M. "Heaven Bound Soldiers: A Negro *Green Pastures*." *ThA*, XV (1931), 855–61.

17 THOMPSON, T. "Burst of Negro Drama." *Life*, LVI (May 29, 1964), 62A–70.

18 TURNER, Darwin T. "The Negro Dramatist's Image of the Universe." *CLAJ*, V (1961), 106–20. (Reprinted in 15.5, 19.11, 30.15.*)

19 TURNER, Darwin T. "Negro Playwrights and the Urban Negro." *CLAJ*, XII (1968), 19–25.

20 TURNER, Darwin T. "Past and Present in Negro Drama." *NALF*, II (1968), 26–27.

21 TURPIN, Waters E. "The Contemporary American Negro Playwright." *CLAJ*, IX (1965), 12–24.

22 WARD, Douglas Turner. "Needed: A Theater for Black Themes." *ND*, XVII (December, 1967), 34–39.

23 "Why Not a Negro Drama for Negroes by Negroes?" *CurOp*, LXXII (1922), 639–40.

24 WILLIAMS, Jim. "The Need for a Harlem Theatre." *Freedomways*, III (1963), 307–11.

25 WYATT, E. V. "American Negro Theater." *CathW*, CLI (August, 1945), 432.

Fiction

26 ANGOFF, Allan. "Protest in American Literature since the End of World War II." *CLAJ*, V (1961), 31–40.

27 ARDEN, Eugene. "The Early Harlem Novel." *Phylon*, XX (1959), 25–31.

1 BARCUS, F. Earle and Jack LEVIN. "Role Distance in Negro and Majority Fiction." *JQ*, XLIII (1966), 709–14.

2 BARKSDALE, Richard K. "Alienation and the Anti-Hero in Recent American Fiction." *CLAJ*, X (1966), 1–10.*

3 BARTON, Rebecca C. *Race Consciousness and the American Negro: A Study of the Correlation between the Group Experience and the Fiction of 1900–1930.* Copenhagen: Busck, 1934.

4 BLAND, Edward. "Social Forces Shaping the Negro Novel." *NQ*, I (1945), 241–48.

5 BONE, Robert A. *The Negro Novel in America.* Rev. ed. New Haven, Conn.: Yale UP, 1965. (Bibliography.)*†

6 BRAWLEY, Benjamin. "The Negro in American Fiction." *Dial*, LX (1916), 445–50.

7 BROWN, Sterling. *The Negro in American Fiction.* Washington, D.C.: Associates in Negro Folk Education, 1937. (Bibliography.)*

8 BUTCHER, Philip. "The Younger Novelists and the Urban Negro." *CLAJ*, IV (1961), 196–203.

9 BYRD, James W. "Stereotypes of White Characters in Early Negro Novels." *CLAJ*, I (1957), 28–35.

10 CHANDLER, G. Lewis. "Coming of Age: A Note on American Negro Novelists." *Phylon*, IX (1948), 25–29.

11 CHANDLER, G. Lewis. "A Major Problem of Negro Authors in Their March toward Belles-Lettres." *Phylon*, XI (1950), 383–86.

12 CHAPMAN, Abraham. See 22.19.

13 CLARKE, John Henrik. "Transition in the American Negro Short Story." *Phylon*, XXI (1960), 360–66.

14 COTHRAN, Tilman C. "White Stereotypes in Fiction by Negroes." *Phylon*, XI (1950), 252–56.

15 DAYKIN, Walter I. "Social Thought in Negro Novels." *S&SR*, XIX (1935), 247–52.

16 ELLISON, Ralph. "Recent Negro Fiction." *New Masses*, XL (August 5, 1941), 22–25.

17 FIEDLER, Leslie. *Love and Death in the American Novel.* Rev. ed. New York: Stein & Day, 1966.†

18 FORD, Nick Aaron. *The Contemporary Negro Novel, a Study in Race Relations.* Boston: Meador, 1936.

19 FRAZIER, E. Franklin. "The God of Fiction." *Colorado Quarterly*, VII (1958), 207–220.

20 FULLER, Hoyt W. "Contemporary Negro Fiction." *SWR*, L (1965), 321–35.*

21 GÉRARD, Albert. "Humanism and Negritude: Notes on the Contemporary Afro-American Novel." *Diogenes*, XXXVII (1962), 115–33.

22 GLICKSBERG, Charles I. "Bias, Fiction, and the Negro." *Phylon*, XIII (1952), 127–35.

23 GLICKSBERG, Charles I. "The Furies in Negro Fiction." *WestR*, XIII (1949), 107–14.

1   GLICKSBERG, Charles I. "The Negro Cult of the Primitive." *AR*, IV (1944), 47–55.

2   GLICKSBERG, Charles I. "Negro Fiction in America." *SAQ*, XLV (1946), 477–88.

3   GLOSTER, Hugh M. *Negro Voices in American Fiction.* Chapel Hill: U of North Carolina P, 1948.*

4   GREEN, Gerald. "Back to Bigger." *KR*, XXVIII (1966), 521–39. (Current novels.)

5   GRIMER, Alan and Janet OWEN. "Civil Rights and the Race Novel." *CJF*, XV (1956), 12–15.

6   GROSS, Seymour. See 1.13, 24.10.*

7   HOWE, Irving. "Black Boys and Native Sons." *Dissent*, X (1963), 353–68. (Baldwin, Ellison, Wright.)

8   HOWE, Irving and Ralph ELLISON. "The Writer and the Critic—An Exchange." *NeL*, XLVI (February 3, 1964). (Howe's essay is reprinted in *A World More Attractive.* New York: Horizon, 1963; Ellison's is reprinted in 6.14.)

9   HUGGINS, Kathryn. "Aframerican Fiction." *Southern Literary Messenger*, III (1941), 315–20.

10 HUGHES, Carl Milton. *The Negro Novelist.* New York: Citadel, 1953.

11 JACKSON, Blyden. "A Golden Mean for the Negro Novel." *CLAJ*, III (1959), 81–87.

12 JACKSON, Blyden. "The Negro's Image of the Universe as Reflected in His Fiction." *CLAJ*, IV (1960), 22–31. (Reprinted in 15.5.)

13 JACKSON, Blyden. "The Negro's Negro in Negro Literature." *MQR*, IV (1965), 290–95.*

14 JARRETT, Thomas. "Recent Fiction by Negroes." *CE*, XVI (1954), 85–91.

15 JARRETT, Thomas. "Toward Unfettered Creativity: A Note on the Negro Novelist's Coming of Age." See 27.19, pp. 313–17.

16 KENT, George E. "Ethnic Impact in American Literature: Reflections on a Course." *CLAJ*, XI (1967), 24–37.

17 KNOX, George. "The Negro Novelist's Sensibility and the Outsider Theme." *WHR*, XI (1957), 137–48.

18 LEHAN, Richard. "Existentialism in Recent American Fiction: The Demonic Quest." *TSLL*, I (1959), 181–202.

19 MARCUS, Steven. See 27.9.

20 MAUND, Alfred. See 27.12.

21 MEIER, August. "Some Reflections on the Negro Novel." *CLAJ*, II (1959), 168–77. (Critical review of Bone's *Negro Novel in America*.)*

22 MULDER, Arnold. "Wanted: A Negro Novelist." *Independent*, CXII (1924), 341–42.

23 MURRAY, Albert. "Something Different, Something More." See 24.14, pp. 112–37. (Protest fiction.)

24 REDDICK, L. D. "No Kafka in the South." See 27.19, pp. 380–83.

25 REDDING, Saunders. See 28.12.

26 STARKE, Juanita. "Symbolism of the Negro College in Three Recent Novels." *Phylon*, XVII (1956), 365–73.

27 TURNER, Darwin T. "*The Negro Novel in America: In Rebuttal.*" *CLAJ*, X (1966), 122–34. (Reprinted as "The Literary Presumptions of Mr. Bone," *ND*, XVI (August, 1967), 54–65.)*

1 TURNER, Darwin T. "The Negro Novelist and the South." *SHR*, I (1967), 21–29.*

2 TURPIN, Waters E. "Four Short Fiction Writers of the Harlem Renaissance—Their Legacy of Achievement." *CLAJ*, XI (1967), 59–72. (Toomer, Fisher, Hughes, McKay.)

3 WARFEL, Harry R. *American Novelists of Today.* New York: American, 1951.

4 WINSLOW, Henry. "Two Visions of Reality." *ND*, XVI (May, 1967), 36–39.

Poetry

5 BARKSDALE, Richard K. "Trends in Contemporary Poetry." *Phylon*, XIX (1958), 408–16.*

6 BENNETT, M. W. "Negro Poets." *NHB*, IX (1946), 171–72, 191.

7 BERGER, Art. "Negroes with Pens." *Mainstream*, XVI (July, 1963), 3–6.

8 BLAND, Edward. "Racial Bias and Negro Poetry." *Phylon*, LXIII (1944), 328–33.

9 BONTEMPS, Arna. "American Negro Poetry." *C*, LXX (1963), 509.

10 BONTEMPS, Arna. "Negro Poets, Then and Now." See 27.19, pp. 355–60.

11 BROOKS, Gwendolyn. "Poets Who Are Negro." See 27.19, p. 312.

12 BROWN, Sterling A. See 16.4, 16.5, 29.21.

13 BROWN, Sterling A. *Outline for the Study of the Poetry of American Negroes.* New York: Harcourt, Brace, 1931. (To be used with *The Book of American Negro Poetry.* See 20.7.)*

14 CHARTERS, Samuel B. See 9.12.

15 COLLIER, Eugenia W. "I Do Not Marvel, Countee Cullen." *CLAJ*, XI (1967), 73–87. (Negro poets.)

16 DAYKIN, Walter I. "Race Consciousness in Negro Poetry." *S&SR*, XX (1936), 98–105.

17 ECHERUO, M. J. C. "American Negro Poetry." *Phylon*, XXIV (1963), 62–68.

18 GARRETT, Naomi M. "Racial Motifs in Contemporary American and French Negro Poetry." *WVUPP*, XIV (1963), 80–101.

19 GLICKSBERG, Charles I. "Negro Poets and the American Tradition." *AR*, VI (1946), 243–53.

20 JOHNSON, Charles S. "Jazz Poetry and Blues." See 22.17, pp. 16–20.

21 JOHNSON, James W. See 20.7.

22 LOCKE, Alain. "The Message of the Negro Poets." See 22.17, pp. 5–15.

23 MONROE, Harriet. "Negro Sermon Poetry." *Phylon*, XXX (1923), 291–93.

24 MOORE, Rayburn S. "Thomas Dun's English, A Forgotten Contributor to the Development of Negro Dialect Verse in the 1870's." *AL*, XXXIII (1961), 72–75.

25 MORPURGO, J. E. "American Negro Poetry." *Fortnightly*, CLXVIII (July, 1947), 16–24.

26 POOL, Rosey. "The Discovery of American Negro Poetry." *Freedomways*, III (1963), 46–51.

1   PREMINGER, Alex, Frank J. WARNK and O. B. HARDISON Jr., eds. "Negro Poetry." *Encyclopedia of Poetry and Poetics*. Princeton: Princeton UP, 1965.

2   ROLLINS, Charlemae. *Famous American Negro Poets*. New York: Dodd, Mead, 1965. (For children.)

3   TAUSSEG, Charlotte E. "The New Negro as Revealed in His Poetry." *O*, V (1927), 108–11.

4   THURMAN, Wallace. "Negro Poets and Their Poetry." *Bookman*, LXVII (1928), 555–61.

5   "The Umbra Poets." *Mainstream*, XVI (July, 1963), 7–13. (Selections from contemporary urban poets, including Calvin Hernton.)

6   WAGNER, Jean. *Les poètes nègres des États-Unis: Le sentiment racial et religeux dans la poésie de P. L. Dunbar à L. Hughes*. Paris: Istra, 1963.

7   WALKER, Margaret. "New Poets." See 27.19, pp. 345–54.

8   WHITE, Newman. "American Negro Poetry." *SAQ*, XX (1921), 304–22.

9   WHITE, Newman. "Racial Feeling in Negro Poetry." *SAQ*, XXI (1922), 14–29.

10   WRIGHT, Richard. "Littérature noire américaine." *Temps M*, IV (1948), 193–221. (History of Negro American poets.)

Folklore

Emphasis in this section is given to books in which folklore of Afro-Americans is used, compiled, or discussed. Articles and short tales not included in collections have been excluded except when they are of unusual interest or significance or when they represent the work of individuals who have earned distinction for their use or compilation of such folklore.

11   BONTEMPS, Arna and Langston HUGHES, eds. *The Book of Negro Folklore*. New York: Dodd, Mead, 1958.*

12   BREWER, J. Mason. "American Negro Folklore." *Phylon*, VI (1945), 354–61.*

13   BREWER, J. Mason. *American Negro Folklore*. Chicago: Quadrangle, 1968.*†

14   BREWER, J. Mason. "*Aunt Dicy*" Tales. Austin, Texas: The Author, 1957.

15   BREWER, J. Mason. "*Dog Ghosts*" *and Other Texas Negro Folk Tales*. Austin: U of Texas P, 1958.

16   BREWER, J. Mason. "Negro Folklore in North America." *NMQ*, XVI (1946), 47–48.

17   BREWER, J. Mason. *The Word on the Brazos*. Austin: U of Texas P, 1953.*

18   BREWER, J. Mason. *Worser Days and Better Times: The Folklore of the North Carolina Negro*. Chicago: Quadrangle, 1965.*

19   BROOKES, Stella Brewer. *Joel Chandler Harris, Folklorist*. Athens: U of Georgia P, 1950.†

20   BROWN, Sterling A. "Negro Folk Expression." See 27.19, pp. 318–27.

21   BROWN, W. N. "Hindu Stories in American Negro Folklore." *Asia*, XXI (1921), 703–7.

1 BYRD, James W. *J. Mason Brewer: Negro Folklorist.* Austin, Texas: Steck-Vaughn, 1967.

2 CLARK, Kenneth. "Folklore of Negro Children in Greater Louisville Reflecting Attitudes toward Race." *KFR*, X (1964), 1–11.

3 CROWLEY, Daniel J. "Negro Folklore: An Africanist's View." *TQ*, VII (1962), 65–71.

4 DAVIS, H. C. "Negro Folklore in South Carolina." *JAF*, (1914), 241–54.

5 DORSON, Richard M. "The Career of John Henry." *WF*, XXIV (1965), 155–63.

6 DORSON, Richard M. "A French Look at Negro Storytelling." *ArF*, XVI (August 15, 1953), 2–3.

7 DORSON, Richard M. *Negro Folktales in Michigan.* Cambridge, Mass.: Harvard UP, 1956.*

8 DORSON, Richard M. "A Negro Storytelling Session on Tape." *MidF*, II (1953), 201–12.

9 DORSON, Richard M. "Negro Tales." *WF*, XIII (1954), 77–97, 160–69.

10 DORSON, Richard M. *Negro Tales from Pine Bluff, Arkansas, and Calvin, Michigan.* Bloomington: Indiana UP, 1958.*

11 DORSON, Richard M. "Negro Witch Stories on Tape." *MidF*, II (1952), 229–41.

12 ELLIS, A. B. "Evolution in Folklore: Some West African Prototypes of the Uncle Remus Stories." *PopSc*, XLVIII (November, 1895), 93–104.

13 FAUSET, Arthur Huff. "American Negro Folklore." See 12.25, pp. 238–44.*

14 GERBER, A. J. "Uncle Remus Traced to the Old World." *JAF*, VI (1895), 245.

15 HARRIS, Joel C. *Daddy Jake the Runaway, and Short Stories told after Dark.* New York: Century, 1889.

16 HARRIS, Joel C. *Nights with Uncle Remus: Myths and Legends of the Old Plantation.* Boston: Osgood, 1883.

17 HARRIS, Joel C. *Tar-Baby, and Other Rhymes of Uncle Remus.* New York: Appleton, 1904.

18 HARRIS, Joel C. *Told by Uncle Remus; New Stories of the Old Plantation.* New York: McClure, Phillips, 1905.

19 HARRIS, Joel C. *Uncle Remus and Brer Rabbit.* New York: Stokes, 1906.

20 HARRIS, Joel C. *Uncle Remus and his Friends: Old Plantation Stories, Songs and Ballads, with Sketches of Negro Character.* Boston: Houghton, Mifflin, 1892.

21 HARRIS, Joel C. *Uncle Remus and the Little Boy.* Boston: Small, Maynard, 1910. (A collection of stories and rhymes appearing in *Uncle Remus' Magazine* during 1907 and 1908.)

22 HARRIS, Joel C. *Uncle Remus, His Songs and His Sayings.* New York: Appleton, 1880.

23 HARRIS, Joel C. *Uncle Remus Returns.* Boston: Houghton, Mifflin, 1918. (A collection of stories and sketches appearing in the *Metropolitan Magazine*, 1905 and 1906, and *The Atlanta Constitution*.)

24 HAYWOOD, Charles. *A Bibliography of North American Folklore and Folksong.* 2nd ed., rev. New York: Dover, 1961, I, 430–560.

1 HEYWARD, Dubose and Hervey ALLEN. *Carolina Chansons: Legends of the Low Country.* New York: Macmillan, 1922.

2 HUGHES, Langston, ed. *The Book of Negro Humor.* New York: Dodd, Mead, 1966.

3 HURSTON, Zora N. "High John de Conjure; Negro Folklore Offers Solace to Sufferers." *AMer*, LVII (1943), 450–8.

4 HURSTON, Zora N. *Mules and Men.* Philadelphia: Lippincott, 1935.*

5 HURSTON, Zora N. *Tell My Horse.* Philadelphia: Lippincott, 1938.

6 JACKSON, Bruce, comp. *The Negro and His Folklore in Nineteenth Century Periodicals.* Austin: U of Texas P, 1967. (Bibliography.)*

7 JACKSON, Margaret Y. "Folklore in Slave Narratives Before the Civil War." *NYFQ*, XI (April, 1955), 5–19.*

8 JOHNSON, Guy B. *John Henry: Tracking Down a Negro Legend.* Chapel Hill: U of North Carolina P, 1929.

9 KENNEDY, R. Emmett. *Black Cameos.* New York: Boni, 1924.

10 KERRY, L. "Negro Witch Stories on Tape." *MidF*, II (1952), 229–41.

11 LAW, Robert A. "Notes on Some Recent Treatments of Negro Folklore." *TFS*, VII (1927), 140–44.

12 LOMAX, Alan. "'Sinful' Songs of the Southern Negro." *SWR*, XIX (1934), 105–31.

13 PENDLETON, L. "Notes on Negro Folklore and Witchcraft in the South." *JAF*, III (1890), 201–7.

14 PUCKETT, N. N. *Folk Beliefs of the Southern Negro.* Chapel Hill: U of North Carolina P, 1926.

15 SCARBOROUGH, W. W. "Negro Folklore and Dialect." *Arena*, XVII (1897), 186–92.

16 STERLING, Philip. *Laughing on the Outside.* New York: Grosset & Dunlap, 1966. (Anthology of Negro humor.)

17 TALLEY, T. W. *Negro Folk Rhymes, Wise and Otherwise.* New York: Macmillan, 1922.

18 THOMAS, Wright. "Negro Tales from Bolivar Country Mississippi." *SFQ*, XIX (1954), 104–16.

19 WALTON, David A. "Joel Chandler Harris as Folklorist: A Reassessment." *KFQ*, XI (1966), 21–26.

20 WARING, M. A. "Mortuary Customs and Beliefs of South Carolina Negroes." *JAF*, VII (1894), 318–19.

Afro-American Writers

The following list includes all published book-length works in fiction, drama, or poetry by the most significant writers. Cross reference is made to their volumes of essays. Other relevant works of nonfiction by these writers are included in other sections of this bibliography. For less well-known writers, representative works have been listed. Some of the less well-known writers have not received critical or biographical notice. For reviews of their works, see *Book Review Digest* and Arthur Spingarn's reviews in *The Crisis*. For additional biographical material about contemporary authors, see *Contemporary Authors*, *Current Biography*, and *Twentieth Century Authors*.

Anderson, Alston

1 *Lover Man.* Garden City, N.Y.: Doubleday, 1959. (Short stories; author was born in Panama but has been resident of U.S. since 14.)

Attaway, William

2 *Blood on the Forge.* New York: Doubleday, Doran, 1941. (Novel.)

3 *Let Me Breathe Thunder.* New York: Doubleday, Doran, 1939. (Novel.)

BIOGRAPHY AND CRITICISM

4 BONE, Robert. See 31.5.*

5 GLOSTER, Hugh M. See 32.3.

6 MARGOLIES, Edward. See 27.10.

Baldwin, James

7 See 6.3, 6.4, 6.5.*

8 *Another Country.* New York: Dial, 1962. (Novel.)*†

9 *Blues for Mister Charlie.* New York: Dial, 1964. (Drama.)*†

10 *Giovanni's Room.* New York: Dial, 1956. (Novel.)†

11 *Go Tell It on the Mountain.* New York: Knopf, 1953. (Novel.)*†

12 *Going to Meet the Man.* New York: Dial, 1965. (Short stories.)†

13 *Tell Me How Long the Train's Been Gone.* New York: Dial, 1967. (Novel.)†

BIBLIOGRAPHIES

14 FISHER, Russell G. "James Baldwin: A Bibliography, 1947–1962." *BB,* IV (1965), 127–130.

15 KINDT, Kathleen A. "James Baldwin, A Checklist: 1947–1962." *BB,* XXIV (1965), 123–126.

BIOGRAPHY AND CRITICISM

16 ALLEN, Walter. *The Modern Novel in Britain and the United States.* New York: Dutton, 1964.†

17 BARKSDALE, Richard K. "'Temple of the Fire Baptized.'" *Phylon,* XIV (1953), 326–327.

18 BIGBY, C. W. "The Committed Writer: James Baldwin as Dramatist." *TCL,* XIII (1967), 39–48.

1 BOYLE, Kay. "Introducing James Baldwin." *Contemporary American Novelists*. Ed. Harry T. Moore. Carbondale: Southern Illinois UP, 1964.

2 BONE, Robert A. "The Novels of James Baldwin." *Tri-Quarterly*, No. 2 (Winter, 1965), 3–20. (Reprinted in 31.5.)

3 BONOSKY, Phillip. "The Negro Writer and Commitment." *Mainstream*, XV (February, 1962), 16–22.

4 BRADFORD, Melvin E. "Faulkner, James Baldwin, and the South." *GaR*, XX (1966), 431–43.

5 CARTEY, Wilfred. See 22.14.

6 CHARNEY, Maurice. "James Baldwin's Quarrel with Richard Wright." *AQ*, XV (1963), 65–75.

7 CLARK, Kenneth B. "A Conversation with James Baldwin." *Freedomways*, III (1963), 361–68.

8 CLEAVER, Eldridge. "Notes on a Native Son." See 9.8.

9 COLES, Robert. "Baldwin's Burden." *PR*, XXXI (1964), 409–16.

10 COLLIER, Eugenia W. "The Phrase Unbearably Repeated." *Phylon*, XXV (1964), 288–96.

11 COX, C. B. and A. R. JONES. "After the Tranquilized Fifties: Notes on Sylvia Plath and James Baldwin." *CritQ*, VI (1964), 107–22.

12 ECKMAN, Fern M. *The Furious Passage of James Baldwin*. New York: Popular Library, 1967.†

13 ELKOFF, Marvin. "Everybody Knows His Name." *Esquire*, LXII, ii (1964), 59–64, 120–23.

14 FEATHERSTONE, J. "Blues for Mr. Baldwin." *NR*, CLIII (November 27, 1965), 34–36.

15 FINN, James. "The Identity of James Baldwin." *Commonweal*, LXXVII (1962), 113–16, 365–66.

16 FINN, James. "James Baldwin's Vision." *Commonweal*, LXXVII (1962), 447–49.

17 FOOTE, Dorothy N. "James Baldwin's 'Holler Books'." *CEA*, XXV, viii (1963), 8, 11.

18 FRIEDENBERG, Edgar Z. "Another Country for an Arkansas Traveler." *NR*, CXLVII (August 27, 1962), 23–26.

19 FULLER, Hoyt W. See 31.20.

20 GAYLE, Addison. "A Defense of James Baldwin." *CLAJ*, X (1966), 201–8.

21 GÉRARD, Albert. "James Baldwin et la réligiosité noire." *Revue Nouvelle*, XXXIII (1963), 177–186.

22 GRAVES, Wallace. "The Question of Moral Energy in James Baldwin's *Go Tell It on the Mountain*." *CLAJ*, VII (1963), 215–23.

23 GRESSET, Michel. "Sur James Baldwin." *MdF*, CCCL (1964), 653–55.

24 GROSS, Theodore. "The World of James Baldwin." *Critique*, VII, ii (1965), 139–49.

25 HAGOPIAN, John V. "James Baldwin: The Black and the Red-White-and-Blue." *CLAJ*, VII (1963), 133–40.

1   HASSAN, Ihab. "The Novel of Outrage: A Minority Voice in Postwar American Fiction." *AmS*. XXXIV (1965), 239–53.

2   HASSAN, Ihab. *Radical Innocence*. Princeton: Princeton UP, 1961.†

3   HEIBERG, Inger. "James Baldwin—negerforfatter og dikter." *Samtiden*, LXXIV (1965), 280–87.

4   HERNTON, Calvin C. "Blood of the Lamb." See 11.19, pp. 105–47.*

5   HOFFMAN, Stanton. "The Cities of Night: John Rechy's *City of Night* and the American Literature of Homosexuality." *CR*, XVII, ii–iii (1964), 195–206.

6   ISAACS, Harold. See 24.27.

7   JACOBSON, Dan. "James Baldwin as Spokesman." *Commentary*, XXXII (1961), 497–502.

8   KATTAN, Naim. "Deux écrivains américains." *EdCF*, XVII (1964), 87–135.

9   KAZIN, Alfred. "The Essays of James Baldwin." *Contemporaries*. Boston: Little, Brown, 1962, pp. 254–56.

10 KENT, George E. "Baldwin and the Problem of Being." *CLAJ*, VII (1964), 202–14.*

11 KILLENS, John O. See 30.8.

12 KLEIN, Marcus. "James Baldwin." *After Alienation: American Novels in Mid-Century*. Cleveland: World, 1964.*

13 LASH, John S. "Baldwin Beside Himself: A Study in Modern Phallicism." *CLAJ*, VIII (1964), 132–40.

14 LEVANT, Howard. "Aspiraling We Should Go." *MASJ*, IV, ii (1963), 3–20.

15 LEVIN, David. "Baldwin's Autobiographical Essays: The Problem of Negro Identity." *MR*, V (1964), 239–47.

16 MAC INNES, Colin. "Dark Angel: The Writings of James Baldwin." *Encounter*, XXI (August, 1963), 22–33.*

17 MARCUS, Steven. See 27.9.

18 MARKHOLT, Ottilie. "White Critic, Black Playwright: Water and Fire." *ND*, XVI (April, 1967), 54–60.

19 MAYFIELD, Julian. "And Then Came Baldwin." *Freedomways*, III (1963), 143–55.*

20 MOORE, John R. "An Embarrassment of Riches: Baldwin's *Going to Meet the Man*." *HC*, II, v (1965), 1–12.

21 MORRISON, Allan. "The Angriest Young Man." *Ebony*, XVI (October, 1961), 23–30.

22 MURRAY, Albert. "Something Different, Something More." See 24.14.

23 NEWMAN, Charles. "The Lesson of the Master: Henry James and James Baldwin." *YR*, LVI (1966), 45–59.

24 O'DANIEL, Therman B. "James Baldwin: An Interpretive Study." *CLAJ*, VII (1963), 37–47.

25 PETERSEN, Fred. "James Baldwin and Eduardo Mallea: Two Essayists' Search for Identity." *Discourse*, X (1967), 97–107.

1   PODHORETZ, Norman. "In Defense of Baldwin." *Doing and Undoings.* New York: Farrar, Straus, 1964.

2   RADDATZ, Fritz J. "Schwarz ist die Farbe der Einsamkeit: Skizze zu einer Porträt James Baldwin." *FH*, XX (1965), 44–52.

3   RAINER, Dachine. "Rage into Order." *Commonweal*, LXIII (1956), 384–6. (Review of *Notes of a Native Son*.)

4   ROTH, Phillip. "Channel X: Two Plays on the Race Conflict." *NYRB*, II (May 28, 1964), 10–13.

5   SAYRE, Robert F. "James Baldwin's Other Country." *Contemporary American Novelists*. Ed. Harry T. Moore. Carbondale: Southern Illinois UP, 1964, pp. 158–69.

6   SCHROTH, Raymond A. "James Baldwin's Search." *CathW*, CXCVIII (1964), 288–94.

7   SPENDER, Stephen. "James Baldwin: Voice of a Revolution." *PR*, XXX (1963), 256–60.

8   STANDLEY, Fred L. "James Baldwin: The Crucial Situation." *SAQ*, LXV (1966), 371–81.

9   STRONG, Augusta. "Notes on James Baldwin." *Freedomways*, II (1962), 167–71.

10   WATSON, Edward A. "The Novels of James Baldwin: Case-Book of a 'Lover's War' with the United States." *MR*, VI (1965), 385–402.

11   WIISTENHAGEN, Heinz. "James Baldwin's Essays und Romane: Versuch einer ersten Einschatzung." *ZAA*, XIII (1965), 117–57.

Beaumont, Charles

12   *The Intruder*. New York: Putnam, 1959. (Novel.)†

Bell, James Madison

13   *The Poetical Works of James Madison Bell*. 2nd ed. Lansing, Mich.: Wynkoop, Hallenbeck, Crawford, 1901.

BIOGRAPHY AND CRITICISM

14   BRAWLEY, Benjamin. See 19.5.*

15   LOGGINS, Vernon. See 27.8.*

16   REDDING, Saunders. See 28.13.

Bennett, Hal

17   *A Wilderness of Vines*. New York: Doubleday, 1966.

18   *The Black Wine*. New York: Doubleday, 1968.†

Boles, Robert

1 *Curling*. Boston: Houghton Mifflin, 1968.

2 *The People One Knows*. Boston: Houghton Mifflin, 1965.

BIOGRAPHY AND CRITICISM

3 GREENYA, John. "A Colorless Sort of Gray." *SR*, LI (Feb. 17, 1968), 38.

Bontemps, Arna

4 *Black Thunder*. New York: Macmillan, 1936. (Novel.)*†

5 *Chariot in the Sky*. Philadelphia: Winston, 1951.

6 *Drums at Dusk*. New York: Macmillan, 1939. (Novel.)

7 *The Fast Sooner Hound*. Boston: Houghton Mifflin, 1942. (Juvenile fiction.)

8 *God Sends Sunday*. New York: Harcourt, Brace, 1931. (Novel.)

9 *Lonesome Boy*. Boston: Houghton Mifflin, 1955. (Juvenile fiction.)

10 *Personals*. London: Breman, 1963. (Volume 4 in the Heritage series of American Negro poetry.)

11 (Co-authored with Langston HUGHES.) *Popo and Fifina: Children of Haiti*. New York: Macmillan, 1932. (Juvenile.)

12 *Sad-faced Boy*. Boston: Houghton Mifflin, 1937. (Juvenile fiction.)

13 *Sam Patch, the High, Wide and Handsome Jumper*. Boston: Houghton Mifflin, 1951. (Juvenile fiction.)

14 *Slappy Hooper, the Wonderful Sign Painter*. Boston: Houghton Mifflin, 1946. (Juvenile fiction.)

15 *You Can't Pet a Possum*. New York: William Morrow, 1934. (Juvenile fiction.)

BIOGRAPHY AND CRITICISM

16 BONE, Robert. See 31.5.

17 GLOSTER, Hugh M. See 32.3.

Braithwaite, William S.

18 *The Canadian, a Novel*. Boston: Small, Maynard, 1901.

19 *Going Over Tindel, a Novel*. Boston: Brimmer, 1924.

20 *The House of Falling Leaves*. Boston: Luce, 1908. (Poems.)

1 *Lyrics of Life and Love.* Boston: Turner, 1904.

2 *Selected Poems.* New York: Coward-McCann, 1948.*

BIOGRAPHY AND CRITICISM

3 BARTON, Rebecca. See 6.6.

4 BRAWLEY, Benjamin. See 21.21.*

5 REDDING, Saunders. See 28.13.*

6 SPELLMAN, Fronzell. "The Twentieth Century's Greatest Negro Anthologist." *NHB*, XXVI (1963), 137.

Branch, William

(No published texts are available for *In Splendid Error* and *A Medal for Willie*, both dramas.)

BIOGRAPHY AND CRITICISM

7 MITCHELL, Loften. "Three Writers and a Dream." *C*, LXXII (1965), 219–23.

Breechwood, Mary

8 *Memphis Jackson's Son.* Boston: Houghton Mifflin, 1956. (Novel.)

Brewer, J. Mason

9 *Negrito: Negro Dialect Poems of the Southwest.* San Antonio, Tex.: Naylor, 1933.

BIOGRAPHY AND CRITICISM

10 BYRD, James W. See 35.1.

Brooks, Gwendolyn

11 *Annie Allen.* New York: Harper, 1949. (Poems; awarded Pulitzer Prize.)*

12 *The Bean Eaters.* New York: Harper, 1960. (Poems.)*

13 *Bronzeville Boys and Girls.* New York: Harper, 1956. (Poems for children.)

14 *In the Mecca.* New York: Harper & Row, 1968. (Poems.)*

15 *Maud Martha.* New York: Harper, 1953. (Novel.)*†

16 *Selected Poems.* New York: Harper & Row, 1963.*†

17 *A Street in Bronzeville.* New York: Harper, 1945. (Poems.)*

BIOGRAPHY AND CRITICISM

1 BROWN, Frank London. "Chicago's Great Lady of Poetry." *ND*, XI (December, 1961), 53–57.

2 CROCKETT, J. "An Essay on Gwendolyn Brooks." *NHB*, XIX (1955), 37–39.

3 CUTLER, B. "Long Reach, Strong Speech." *Poetry*, CIII (1964), 388–89.

4 DAVIS, Arthur P. "The Black-and-Tan Motif in the Poetry of Gwendolyn Brooks." *CLAJ*, VI (1962), 90–97.

5 DAVIS, Arthur P. "Gwendolyn Brooks: A Poet of the Unheroic." *CLAJ*, VII (1963), 114–25.*

6 EMANUEL, James A. "A Note on the Future of Negro Poetry." *NALF*, I (Fall, 1967), 2–3.

7 KUNITZ, Stanley. "Bronze by Gold." *Poetry*, LXXVI (1950), 52–56.

Brown, Frank L.

8 *Trumbull Park*. Chicago: Regnery, 1959. (Novel.)

Brown, Sterling A.

9 *Southern Road*. New York: Harcourt, Brace, 1932. (Poems.)

BIOGRAPHY AND CRITICISM

10 REDDING, Saunders. See 28.13.

Brown, William Wells

11 *Clotelle: A Tale of the Southern States*. Philadelphia: A. Saifer, 1955. (Facsimile reproduction of 1864 edition of the novel.)

AUTOBIOGRAPHY, BIOGRAPHY, AND CRITICISM

12 See 7.11.

13 *Biography of an American Bondsman, by His Daughter*. Boston: Walcutt, 1855.

14 BONE, Robert. See 31.5.

15 BRAWLEY, Benjamin. See 21.21.

16 FARRISON, W. Edward. "The Origin of Brown's Clotel." *Phylon*, XV (1954), 327–47.*

1 FARRISON, W. Edward. "Phylon Profile XVI, William Wells Brown," *Phylon*, IX (1948), 13–25.*

2 GLOSTER, Hugh. See 32.3.

3 LOGGINS, Vernon. See 27.8.*

4 REDDING, Saunders. See 28.13.*

Chastain, Thomas

5 *Judgment Day.* Garden City, N.Y.: Doubleday, 1962. (Novel.)

Chesnutt, Charles Waddell

6 *The Colonel's Dream.* New York: Doubleday, Page, 1905. (Novel.)

7 *The Conjure Woman and Other Tales.* Boston: Houghton Mifflin, 1899. (Stories.)*

8 *The House Behind the Cedars.* Boston: Houghton Mifflin, 1900. (Novel.)*†

9 *The Marrow of Tradition.* Boston: Houghton Mifflin, 1901. (Novel.)*†

10 *The Wife of His Youth and Other Stories of the Color Line.* New York: Houghton Mifflin, 1899.*†

BIBLIOGRAPHY, BIOGRAPHY, AND CRITICISM

11 AMES, Russell. "Social Realism in Charles Chesnutt." *Phylon*, XIV (1953), 199–206.

12 BONE, Robert. See 31.5.

13 BRAWLEY, Benjamin. See 21.19, 21.21.*

14 CHESNUTT, Helen. *Charles Waddell Chesnutt: Pioneer of the Color Line.* Chapel Hill: U of North Carolina P, 1952.*

15 GLOSTER, Hugh M. "Charles W. Chesnutt: Pioneer in the Fiction of Negro Life." *Phylon*, II (1941), 57–66.*

16 GLOSTER, Hugh M. See 32.3.*

17 HUGHLEY, G. "Charles Waddell Chesnutt." *NHB*, XIX (December, 1955), 54–55.

18 *A List of Manuscripts, Published Works and Related Items in the Charles Chesnutt Collection of the Ernest Milo Cravath Memorial Library.* Nashville, Tenn.: Fisk U Lib., 1954.*

19 LOGGINS, Vernon. See 27.8.

20 MASON, Julian D., Jr. "Charles W. Chesnutt as Southern Author." *Miss Q*, XX (1967), 77–89.

21 PARKER, John W. "Chesnutt as a Southern Town Remembers Him." *C*, LVI (1949), 205–6, 221.

22 REDDING, Saunders. See 28.13.*

23 RENDER, Sylvia Lyons. "Tar Heelia in Chesnutt." *CLAJ*, IX (1965), 39–50.*

1 SMITH, Robert A. "A Note on the Folk Tales of Charles Chesnutt." *CLAJ*, V (1962), 229–32.

2 SILLEN, Samuel. "Charles W. Chesnutt: A Pioneer Negro Novelist." *M&M*, VI (1953), 8–14.*

Childress, Alice

3 *Like One of the Family*. Brooklyn, N.Y.: Independence, 1956. (Novel.)

(No texts are available for *Wedding Band*, produced on Broadway, and other dramas.)

BIOGRAPHY AND CRITICISM

4 MITCHELL, Loften. See 42.7.

Cooper, Clarence L.

5 *The Farm*. New York: Crown, 1967.

BIOGRAPHY AND CRITICISM

6 BARROW, William. "[Review.]" *ND*, XVII (May, 1968), 94–95.

Corrothers, James D.

7 *The Black Cat Club*. New York: Funk & Wagnalls, 1902. (Novel.)

Cotter, Joseph Seamon, Jr.

8 *The Band of Gideon and Other Lyrics*. Boston: Cornhill, 1918.

Cotter, Joseph Seamon, Sr.

9 *Caleb, the Degenerate; a Play in Four Acts. A Study of the Types, Customs and Needs of the American Negro*. New York: Henry Harrison, 1940. (Originally published, 1903.)

10 *Collected Poems of Joseph S. Cotter, Sr*. New York: Harrison, 1938.

11 *Negro Tales*. New York: Cosmopolitan, 1912.

12 *Sequel to the "Pied Piper of Hamelin," and Other Poems*. New York: Harrison, 1939.

13 *A White Song and a Black One*. Louisville, Ky.: Bradley and Gilbert, 1909. (Poems.)

BIOGRAPHY AND CRITICISM

1   BRAWLEY, Benjamin. See 21.21.

2   REDDING, Saunders. See 28.13.

Cullen, Countee

3   *The Ballad of the Brown Girl; an Old Ballad Retold.* New York: Harper, 1927.

4   *The Black Christ and Other Poems.* New York: Harper, 1929.

5   *Color.* New York: Harper, 1925. (Poems.)*

6   *Copper Sun.* New York: Harper, 1927. (Poems.)*

7   *The Lost Zoo; by Countee Cullen and Christopher Cat.* New York: Harper, 1940. (Poems for children.)

8   *The Medea and Other Poems.* New York: Harper, 1935.

9   *My Lives and How I Lost Them; by Christopher Cat in Collaboration with Countee Cullen.* New York: Harper, 1942. (Fiction—autobiography of Christopher Cat.)*

10 *On These I Stand.* New York: Harper, 1947. (Selected Poems.)*

11 *One Way to Heaven.* New York: Harper, 1932. (Novel.)*

BIOGRAPHY AND CRITICISM

12 BONE, Robert. See 31.5.

13 BONTEMPS, Arna. "Countee Cullen, American Poet." *The People's Voice*, V (January 26, 1946), 52–53.

14 BONTEMPS, Arna. See 3.11, 21.13.

15 BRONZ, Stephen A. *Roots of Racial Consciousness; the 1920's: Three Harlem Renaissance Authors.* New York: Libra, 1964.*

16 BROWN, Sterling. See 29.21.

17 DAVIS, Arthur. "The Alien-and-Exile Theme in Countee Cullen's Racial Poems." *Phylon*, XIV (1953), 390–400.*

18 DODSON, Owen. "Countee Cullen (1903–1946)." *Phylon*, VII (1946), 19–21.*

19 FERGUSON, Blanche E. See 23.13.

20 GLOSTER, Hugh M. See 32.3.

21 JOHNSON, Charles, ed. "Countee Cullen." *Source Material for Patterns of Negro Segregation.* Volume VIII. New York: Schomburg Collection.*

22 LASH, John S. "The Anthologist and the Negro Author." *Phylon*, VIII (1947), 68–76.

23 LOCKE, Alain. See 20.14.*

24 PERRY, Margaret. "A Bio-Bibliography of Countee P. Cullen." Washington, D.C.: Catholic U of America, 1959. (Master's thesis.)

1 REDDING, Saunders. See 28.13.*

2 REIMHERR, Beulah. "Countee Cullen: A Biographical and Critical Study." College Part, Maryland: U of Maryland, 1960. (Master's thesis.)*

3 REIMHERR, Beulah. "Race Consciousness in Countee Cullen's Poetry." *SUS*, VII, ii (1963), 65–82.*

4 ROBB, Izetta W. "From the Darker Side." *Opportunity*, IV (1926), 381–82.

5 SMITH, Robert. "The Poetry of Countee Cullen." *Phylon*, XI (1950), 216–21.

6 WEBSTER, Harvey. "A Difficult Career." *Poetry*, LXX (1947), 222–25.

7 WOODRUFF, Bertram. "The Poetic Philosophy of Countee Cullen." *Phylon*, I (1940), 213–23.*

Cuney, Waring

8 *Puzzles*. Selected and introduced by Paul Breman. Utrecht, Holland: Breman, 1961. (Poems.)

Cuney-Hare, Maud

9 *The Message of the Trees; an Anthology of Leaves and Branches*. Boston: Cornhill, 1918.

Davis, Christopher

10 *First Family*. New York: Coward-McCann, 1961. (Novel.)

Davis, Frank Marshall

11 *Black Man's Verse*. Chicago: Black Cat, 1935.

12 *47th Street Poems*. Prairie City, Ill.: Decker, 1948.

13 *I Am the American Negro*. Chicago: Black Cat, 1937.

Davis, Ossie

14 *Purlie Victorious: A Comedy in Three Acts*. New York: French, 1961. [SF.] (Drama.)

Davis, Russell F.

15 *Anything for a Friend*. New York: Crown, 1963. (Novel.)

Delaney, Samuel

1   *Captives of the Flame.* New York: Avon, 1963. (Science fiction.)†
2   *The Tomorrow of Taron.* New York: Avon, 1964. (Science fiction.)†

Demby, William

3   *Beetlecreek.* New York: Rinehart, 1950. (Novel.)*†
4   *The Catacombs.* New York: Pantheon, 1965. (Novel.)

BIOGRAPHY AND CRITICISM

5   BONE, Robert. See 31.5.*
6   MARGOLIES, Edward. See 27.10.

Dodson, Owen

7   *Boy at the Window.* New York: Farrar, Straus, and Young, 1951. (Reprinted as *When Trees Were Green.*) (Novel.)†
8   *Powerful Long Ladder.* New York: Farrar, Straus, 1946. (Poetry.)

BIOGRAPHY AND CRITICISM

9   BONE, Robert. See 31.5.

DuBois, W. E .B.

10   See also 6.12, 6.13.

11   *An ABC of Color: Selections from over a Half-Century of the Writings of W. E. B. DuBois.* Berlin, E. Germany: Seven Seas, 1963.*†

12   *The Black Flame; a Trilogy.* (Book One: *The Ordeal of Mansart,* 1957; Book Two: *Mansart Builds a School,* 1959; Book Three: *Worlds of Color,* 1961.) New York: Mainstream, 1957–61.*†

13   *Dark Princess, a Romance.* New York: Harcourt, Brace, 1928. (Novel.)

14   *Darkwater.* Washington, D.C.: Jenkins, 1920.

15   *The Quest of the Silver Fleece.* Chicago: McClurg, 1911. (Novel.)

16   "Selected Poems of W. E. B. DuBois." *Freedomways,* V (1965), 88–102.*

AUTOBIOGRAPHY, BIOGRAPHY, AND CRITICISM

1 See 6.11.

2 APTHEKER, Herbert. "Some Unpublished Writings of W. E. B. DuBois." *Freedomways*, V (1965), 103–28.

3 BOND, Horace Mann, *et al.* "The Legacy of W. E. B. DuBois." *Freedomways*, V (1965), 16–40.

4 BONE, Robert. See 31.5.

5 BRAWLEY, Benjamin. See 21.19, 21.21.

6 BRODERICK, Francis L. *W. E. B. DuBois, Negro Leader in a Time of Crisis.* Stanford, Calif.: Stanford UP, 1959.*

7 CHAFFEE, M. L. "William E. B. DuBois' Concept of the Racial Problem in the United States." *JNH*, XLI (1956), 241–58.

8 DUBERMAN, M. "DuBois as Prophet." *NR*, CLVIII (1968), 36–39.

9 EMBREE, Edwin R. "W. E. B. DuBois, Elder Statesman." See 10.18.

10 FINKLESTEIN, Sidney. "W. E. B. DuBois' Trilogy: A Literary Triumph." *Mainstream*, XIV (1961), 6–17.

11 GLOSTER, Hugh M. See 32.3.

12 HANSBERRY, William Lee. "W. E. B. DuBois' Influence on African History." *Freedomways*, V (1965), 73–87.

13 HOLMES, Eugene C. "W. E. B. DuBois—Philosopher." *Freedomways*, V (1965), 41–46.

14 HOWE, Irving. "Remarkable Man, Ambiguous Legacy." *Harpers*, CCXXXVI (1968), 143–49,

15 KAISER, Ernest. "A Selected Bibliography of the Published Writings of W. E. B. DuBois." *Freedomways*, V (1965), 207–213.

16 KING, Martin Luther, Jr. "Honoring Dr. DuBois." *Freedomways*, VIII (1968), 104–111.

17 LOVETT, Robert M. "DuBois." *Phylon*, II (1941), 214–18.*

18 REDDING, Saunders. See 28.13.*

19 REDDING, Saunders. "DuBois' Masterpiece Lives on." *Freedomways*, II (1962), 161–164.

20 RUDWICK, Elliott M. *W. E. B. DuBois: A Study in Minority Group Leadership.* Philadelphia: U of Pennsylvania P, 1960. (Reprinted as *W. E. B. DuBois: Propagandist of the Negro Protest*, New York: Atheneum, 1968.)

21 RUDWICK, Elliott M. "W. E. B. DuBois in the Role of Crisis Editor." *JNH*, XLIII (1958), 214–40.

22 THORPE, E. E. "W. E. B. DuBois and Booker T. Washington." *NHB*, XX (November, 1956), 39–42.

23 WESLEY, Charles H. "W. E. B. DuBois, the Historian." *Freedomways*, V (1965), 59–72.

24 "William Edward Burghardt DuBois." *C*, LXX (1963), 468–70.

Dunbar, Paul Laurence

1 BRAWLEY, Benjamin, ed. *The Best Stories of Paul Laurence Dunbar*. New York: Dodd, Mead, 1938.*

2 *The Complete Poems of Paul Laurence Dunbar*, with introduction to *Lyrics of Lowly Life* by W. D. Howells. New York: Dodd, Mead, 1913.*†

3 *The Fanatics*. New York: Dodd, Mead, 1901. (Novel.)

4 *Folks from Dixie*. New York: Dodd, Mead, 1898. (Short stories.)

5 *The Heart of Happy Hollow*. New York: Dodd, Mead, 1904. (Short stories.)

6 *In Old Plantation Days*. New York: Dodd, Mead, 1903. (Short stories.)

7 *The Love of Landry*. New York: Dodd, Mead, 1900. (Novel.)

8 *Lyrics of the Hearthside*. New York: Dodd, Mead, 1899.

9 *Lyrics of Love and Laughter*. New York: Dodd, Mead, 1903.

10 *Lyrics of Lowly Life*. New York: Dodd, Mead, 1896.*

11 *Lyrics of Sunshine and Shadow*. New York: Dodd, Mead, 1905.

12 *Majors and Minors*. Toledo, Ohio: Hadley and Hadley, 1895. (Poems; actually published 1896.)

13 *Oak and Ivy*. Dayton, Ohio: United Brethren, 1893. (Poems; actually published 1892.)

14 *The Sport of the Gods*. New York: Dodd, Mead, 1902. (Novel.)

15 *The Strength of Gideon and Other Stories*. New York: Dodd, Mead, 1900.*

16 *The Uncalled*. New York: Dodd, Mead, 1898. (Novel.)*

17 WIGGINS, Lida Keck, comp. *The Life and Works of Paul Laurence Dunbar*. Naperville, Ill.: Nichols, 1907.

BIBLIOGRAPHY, BIOGRAPHY, AND CRITICISM

18 ACHILLE, L. T. "Paul Laurence Dunbar: poète nègre." *Revue Anglo-Americain*, XII (1934), 504–20.

19 ARNOLD, Edward F. "Some Personal Reminiscences of Dunbar." *JNH*, XVII (1932), 400–408.

20 BONE, Robert. See 31.5.

21 BRAWLEY, Benjamin. "Dunbar Thirty Years After." *SW*, LIX (April, 1930).

22 BRAWLEY, Benjamin. *Paul Laurence Dunbar: Poet of His People*. Chapel Hill: U of North Carolina P, 1936.*

23 BRAWLEY, Benjamin. See 21.19, 21.21.

24 BROWN, Sterling. See 29.21.

1 BURCH, Charles E. "Dunbar's Poetry in Literary English." *SoW*, L (1921), 469–473.

2 BURRIS, Andrew M. "Bibliography of Works by Paul Laurence Dunbar, Negro Poet and Author." *The American Collector*, V (November, 1927.)

3 BUTCHER, Philip. "A Mutual Appreciation: Dunbar and Cable." *CLAJ*, I (1958), 101–102. (Reprinted from *The Free Lance*, IV, i (1947), 2–3.)

4 CLARK, D. W. "Paul Laurence Dunbar." *African Methodist Review*, IV (1906), 555–564.

5 COLLIER, Eugenia. "James Weldon Johnson: Mirror of Change." *Phylon*, XXI (1960), 351–359.

6 CORROTHERS, James D. See 9.19.

7 CUNNINGHAM, Virginia. *Paul Laurence Dunbar and His Song*. New York: Dodd, Mead, 1947.*

8 DANIEL, T. W. "Paul Laurence Dunbar and the Democratic Ideal." *NHB*, VI (1943), 206–8.

9 DUNBAR, Alice. "The Poet and His Song." *AME Church Review*, XII (1914), 121–135.*

10 FORD, Thomas W. See 23.20.

11 GLOSTER, Hugh M. See 32.3.

12 HOWELLS, Mildred, ed. *Life in Letters of William Dean Howells*. Garden City, N.Y.: Doubleday, Doran, 1928.

13 HOWELLS, William Dean. "Life and Letters." *Harpers*, LXIV (1896), 630.

14 HOWELLS, William Dean. "Paul Laurence Dunbar." *North American Review*, XXIII (1906), 185–86.

15 LAWSON, Victor. *Dunbar Critically Examined*. Washington, D.C.: Associated Pub., 1941.*

16 LOGGINS, Vernon. See 27.8.

17 JOHNSON, James W. See 20.7.

18 REDDING, Saunders. See 28.13.

19 STRONKS, James B. "Paul Laurence Dunbar and William Dean Howells." *Ohio History Quarterly*, LXVIII (1957), 95–108.*

20 TURNER, Darwin T. "Paul Laurence Dunbar: The Rejected Symbol." *JNH*, LII (1967), 1–13.*

21 WAGNER, Jean. See 34.6.

22 WALKER, Allen. "Paul Dunbar, A Study in Genius." *PsyR*, XXV (January, 1938).

23 WIGGINS, Lida Keck. See 50.17.

Edmonds, Randolph

24 *Shades and Shadows*. Boston: Meador, 1930. (Plays.)

1 *Six Plays for a Negro Theatre.* Boston: Baker, 1934.

2 *The Land of Cotton and Other Plays.* Washington, D.C.: Associated Pub., 1942. (Also contains *Gangsters Over Harlem; Yellow Death; Silas Brown;* and *The High Court of Historia.*)

Edwards, Junius

3 *If We Must Die.* Garden City, N.Y.: Doubleday, 1963. (Novel.)

Ellison, Ralph

4 Essays. See 6.14.

5 *The Invisible Man.* New York: Random, 1952. (Novel.)*†

BIOGRAPHY AND CRITICISM

6 ALLEN, Walter. See 37.16.

7 BAUMBACK, Jonathan. "Nightmare of a Native Son: Ellison's *Invisible Man.*" *Criticism,* VI (1963), 48–65. (Reprinted in *The Landscape of Nightmare: Studies in the Contemporary American Novel.* New York: New York UP, 1965.)*

8 BENNETT, John Z. "The Race & the Runner: Ellison's *Invisible Man.*" *XUS,* V (1966), 12–26.

9 BLOCK, Alice. "Sight Imagery in *Invisible Man.*" *EJ,* LV (1966), 1019–21, 1024.

10 BLUESTEIN, Gene. "The Blues as Literary Theme." *MR,* VIII (1967), 593–617.

11 BONE, Robert. See 31.5.*

12 BONE, Robert. "Ralph Ellison and the Uses of Imagination." See 24.14, pp. 86–111.*

13 DE LISSOVOY, P. "The Visible Ellison." *Nation,* CXCIX (1964), 334–36.

14 DUPEE, F. W. "On *Invisible Man.*" *Sunday Herald Tribune,* September 26, 1965, pp. 4, 26, 27.*

15 ELLISON, Ralph. See 23.11, 23.12.*

16 ELLISON, Ralph. "Light on *Invisible Man.*" *C,* LX (1953), 157–158.*

17 ELLISON, Ralph. "On Becoming a Writer." *Commentary,* XXXVIII, (1964), 57–60.*

18 EMANUEL, James A. "The Invisible Men of American Literature." *BA,* XXXVI (1963), 391–94.

19 FORD, Nick Aaron. "Four Popular Negro Novelists." *Phylon,* XV (1954), 29–39. (Yerby, Motley, Ellison, Wright.)

20 GELLER, Allen. "An Interview with Ralph Ellison." *TamR,* No. 32, 3–24.

21 GÉRARD, Albert. "Ralph Ellison et le dilemme noir (Le roman afro-américain)." *RGB,* XCVII (1961), 89–104.

22 GLICKSBERG, Charles I. "The Symbolism of Vision." *SWR,* XXXIX (1954), 259–65.

1   HASSAN, Ihab. See 39.1, 39.2.*

2   HOROWITZ, Floyd Ross. "The Enigma of Ellison's Intellectual Man." *CLAJ*, VII (1963), 126–32.

3   HOROWITZ, Floyd Ross. "Ralph Ellison's Modern Version of Brer Bear and Brer Rabbit in *Invisible Man.*" *MASJ*, IV, (1963), 21–27.*

4   ISAACS, Harold. See 24.27.

5   JACKSON, Esther. See 25.8.

6   KLEIN, Marcus. "Ralph Ellison." *After Alienation.* Cleveland: World, 1964. See 39.12.*

7   KOSTELANETZ, Richard. "The Negro Genius." *TC*, MXXXIII (1967), 49–50.

8   KOSTELANETZ, Richard. "The Politics of Ellison's Booker: *Invisible Man* as Symbolic History." *ChiR*, XIX, ii (1967), 5–26.

9   LEE, L. L. "The Proper Self: Ralph Ellison's *Invisible Man.*" *Descant*, X (Spring, 1966), 38–48.

10 LEHAN, Richard. "The Strange Silence of Ralph Ellison." *CEJ*, I, ii, (1965), 63–68.

11 LEVANT, Howard. See 39.14.

12 MARGOLIES, Edward. See 27.10.

13 MENGLING, Marvin E. "Whitman and Ellison: Older Symbols in a Modern Mainstream." *WWR*, XII (1966), 67–70.

14 O'DANIEL, Therman B. "The Image of Man as Portrayed by Ralph Ellison." *CLAJ*, X (1967), 277–284.

15 OLDERMAN, Raymond M. "Ralph Ellison's Blues and *Invisible Man.*" *WSCL*, VII (1966), 142–59.

16 "Ralph Ellison—Fiction Winner." *C*, LX (1953), 154–56.

17 RANDALL, John H., III. "Ralph Ellison: Invisible Man." *RLV*, XXXI (1965), 24–45.

18 ROGGE, Heinz. "Die Amerikanische Negerfrage im Lichte der Literatur von Richard Wright und Ralph Ellison." *NS*, XV (1958), 56–69, 103–17.

19 ROVIT, Earl H. "Ralph Ellison and the American Comic Tradition." *WSCL*, I (1960), 34–42.*

20 WARREN, Robert Penn. "The Unity of Experience." *Commentary*, XXXIX (1965), 91–96.

Emanuel, James A.

21 *The Treehouse and Other Poems.* Detroit: Broadside, 1968.†

Fair, Ronald L.

22 *Hog Butcher.* New York: Harcourt, Brace & World, 1966. (Novel.)

23 *Many Thousand Gone.* New York: Harcourt, Brace & World, 1965. (Novel.)

Fauset, Jessie Redmond

1 *Comedy: American Style.* New York: Stokes, 1933. (Novel.)

2 *Plum Bun.* New York: Stokes, 1929. (Novel.)

3 *The Chinaberry Tree.* New York: Stokes, 1933. (Novel.)*

4 *There Is Confusion.* New York: Boni & Liveright, 1924. (Novel.)

BIOGRAPHY AND CRITICISM

5 BRAITHWAITE, William. "The Novels of Jessie Fauset." *O*, XII (1934), 24–28.*

6 BONE, Robert. See 31.5.

7 GLOSTER, Hugh. See 32.3.*

Fisher, Rudolph

8 *The Walls of Jericho.* New York and London: Knopf, 1928. (Novel.)

9 *The Conjure Man Dies.* New York: Covici-Friede, 1932. (Novel.)

BIOGRAPHY AND CRITICISM

10 BONE, Robert. See 31.5.

11 GLOSTER, Hugh. See 32.3.

Fisher, William

12 *The Waiters.* Cleveland: World, 1953. (Novel.)

Gaines, Ernest J.

13 *Bloodline.* New York: Dial, 1968. (Short stories.)

14 *Catherine Carmier.* New York: Atheneum, 1964. (Novel.

15 *Of Love and Dust.* New York: Dial, 1967. (Novel.)†

BIOGRAPHY AND CRITICISM

1 FULLER, Hoyt W. See 31.20.

2 FULLER, Hoyt W. "Books Noted." *ND*, XVII (Nov., 1967), 51–52, 85.

Griggs, Sutton E.

3 *Imperium in Imperio.* Cincinnati, Ohio: Editor, 1899. (Novel.)

4 *Pointing the Way.* Nashville, Tenn.: Orion, 1908. (Novel.)

5 *Overshadowed.* Nashville, Tenn.: Orion, 1901. (Novel.)

6 *The Hindered Hand, or the Reign of the Repressionist.* Nashville, Tenn.: Orion, 1905. (Novel.)

7 *Triumph of Simple Virtues.* Hot Springs, Ark.: Messenger, 1926.

8 *Unfettered.* Nashville, Tenn.: Orion, 1902. (Novel.)

9 *Wisdom's Call.* Nashville, Tenn.: Orion, 1909.

BIOGRAPHY AND CRITICISM

10 BONE, Robert. See 31.5.

11 GLOSTER, Hugh. See 32.3.*

12 GLOSTER, Hugh. "The Negro in American Fiction . . . Sutton E. Griggs, Novelist of the New Negro." *Phylon*, IV (1943), 335–45.

13 LOGGINS, Vernon. See 27.8.

Grimké, Angelina

14 *Rachel, a Play in Three Acts.* Boston: Cornhill, 1920.

Guy, Rosa B.

15 *Bird at My Window.* Philadelphia: Lippincott, 1966. (Novel.)

Hammon, Jupiter

16 (Poetry available in 19.9, 20.5, 20.7.)

BIOGRAPHY AND CRITICISM

17 BRAWLEY, Benjamin. See 19.5.

1 LOGGINS, Vernon. See 27.8.

2 REDDING, Saunders. See 28.13.

3 WEGELIN, Oscar. *Jupiter Hammon: American Negro Poet.* New York: Heartman, 1915. (Bibliography.)*

Hansberry, Lorraine

4 *A Raisin in the Sun.* New York: Random, 1959. (Drama.)†

5 *The Sign in Sidney Brustein's Window.* New York: Random, 1965. (Drama; intro. to Random House ed. gives history of production.)*†

BIOGRAPHY AND CRITICISM

6 ISAACS, Harold. See 24.27.

7 KILLENS, John O. See 30.8.

8 LEWIS, Theophilus. "Social Protest in *A Raisin in the Sun.*" *CathW*, CXC (1959), 31–35.

9 "Playwright." *New Yorker*, XXXV (May 9, 1959), 33–35.

Harper, Frances Ellen Watkins

10 *Idylls of the Bible.* Philadelphia: The Author, 1906.

11 *Iola Leroy, or Shadows Uplifted.* Philadelphia: Garrigues, 1893. (Novel.)

12 *Moses: A Story of the Nile.* 2nd ed. Philadelphia: Merrihew, 1869.

13 *Poems.* Philadelphia: Ferguson, 1895.

14 *Poems on Miscellaneous Subjects.* Philadelphia: Merrihew, 1874.

15 *Sketches of Southern Life.* Philadelphia: Ferguson, 1888.

BIOGRAPHY AND CRITICISM

16 BRAWLEY, Benjamin. See 19.5.

17 BRAWLEY, Benjamin. "Three Negro Poets: Horton, Mrs. Harper and Whitman." *JNH*, II (1917), 384–92.*

18 GLOSTER, Hugh. See 32.3.

19 LOGGINS, Vernon. See 27.8.*

20 REDDING, Saunders. See 28.13.

Hayden, Robert E.

21 *A Ballad of Remembrance.* London: Breman, 1962. (Poems.)*

1 *Heart-Shape in the Dust*. Detroit: Falcon, 1940. (Poems.)

2 *The Lion and the Archer*. New York: Hemphill, 1949. (Poems.)

3 *Selected Poems*. New York: October House, 1966. (Poems.)

BIOGRAPHY AND CRITICISM

4 GALLER, D. "Three Recent Volumes." *Poetry*, CX (1967), 268.

5 *NHB*, XXI (October, 1957), 15. (Biographical sketch, portrait.)

6 POOL, Rosey E. "Robert Hayden: Poet Laureate." *ND*, XV (June, 1966), 39–43.

Henderson, George Wylie

7 *Jule*. New York: Creative Age, 1946. (Novel.)

8 *Ollie Miss*. New York: Stokes, 1935. (Novel.)*

BIOGRAPHY AND CRITICISM

9 BONE, Robert. See 31.5*

10 GLOSTER, Hugh. See 32.3.

11 TURNER, Darwin T. See 33.1.

Hill, Leslie Pinckney

12 *Toussaint L'Ouverture, a Dramatic History*. Boston: Christopher, 1928.

13 *Wings of Oppression and Other Poems*. Boston: Stratford, 1921.

Hill, Roy L.

14 *49 Poems*. Manhattan, Kansas: Ag Press, 1968.

Himes, Chester

15 *All Shot Up*. New York: Berkeley, 1960. (Novel.)†

16 *The Big Gold Dream*. New York: Berkeley, 1960. (Novel.)†

17 *Cast the First Stone*. New York: Coward-McCann, 1952. (Novel.)

18 *Cotton Comes to Harlem*. New York: Putnam, 1965. (Novel.)†

19 *The Crazy Kill*. New York: Berkeley, 1959. (Novel.)†

20 *For the Love of Imabelle*. Greenwich, Conn.: Fawcett, 1957. (Novel.)

21 *The Heat's On*. New York: Putnam, 1966. (Novel.)†

1   *If He Hollers Let Him Go.* New York: Doubleday, Doran, 1945. (Novel.)*†

2   *Lonely Crusade.* New York: Knopf, 1947. (Novel.)

3   *Pinktoes.* New York: Putnam, 1965. (Novel.)†

4   *The Primitive.* New York: New American Library, 1955. (Novel.)

5   *A Rage in Harlem.* New York: Avon, 1965. (Novel.)

6   *The Real Cool Killers.* New York: Berkeley, 1959. (Novel.)†

7   *Run Man Run.* New York: Putnam, 1966. (Novel.)†

8   *The Third Generation.* New York: World, 1954. (Novel.)*†

BIOGRAPHY AND CRITICISM

9   BONE, Robert. See 31.5.

10   "Chester Himes." *Encyclopedia International.* 2nd ed. New York: Grolier 1968.

11   MARGOLIES, Edward. See 27.10.

Holder, Geoffrey

12   *Black Gods, Green Islands.* N.Y.: Doubleday, 1959. (Novel.)

Horne, Frank

13   *Haverstraw.* London: Breman, 1963. (Poems.)

Horton, George Moses

14   *Poems by a Slave.* See 75.14.

BIOGRAPHY AND CRITICISM

15   BRAWLEY, Benjamin. See 19.5, 56.17.

16   LOGGINS, Vernon. See 27.8.

17   REDDING, Saunders. See 28.13.

18   WALSER, Richard. *The Black Poet.* New York: Philosophical Library, 1967.*

Hughes, Langston

19   *Ask Your Mama: 12 Moods for Jazz.* New York: Knopf, 1961. (Poems.)

20   *The Best of Simple.* New York: Hill and Wang, 1961. (Short stories.)*†

21   *The Dream Keeper and Other Poems.* New York: Knopf, 1932.

1 *Fields of Wonder*. New York: Knopf, 1947. (Poems.)

2 *Fine Clothes to the Jew*. New York: Knopf, 1927. (Poems.)*

3 *Five Plays by Langston Hughes*. Ed. Webster Smalley. Bloomington: Indiana UP, 1963. (*Mulatto, Soul Gone Home, Little Ham, Simply Heavenly*, and *Tambourines to Glory*.)*

4 *The Langston Hughes Reader*. New York: Braziler, 1958.*

5 *The Langston Hughes Reader*. New York: Dodd, Mead, 1966.*

6 *Laughing to Keep from Crying*. New York: Holt, 1952. (Short stories.)*

7 *Montage of a Dream Deferred*. New York: Holt, 1951. (Poems.)*

8 *Not Without Laughter*. New York: Knopf, 1930. (Novel.)*

9 *One-Way Ticket*. New York: Knopf, 1949. (Poems.)

10 *The Panther and the Lash: Poems of Our Times*. New York: Knopf, 1967.

11 *Scottsboro Limited: Four Poems and a Play in Verse*. New York: Golden Stair, 1932.

12 *The Selected Poems of Langston Hughes*. New York: Knopf, 1965.*

13 *Shakespeare in Harlem*. New York: Knopf, 1942. (Poems.)

14 *Simple Speaks His Mind*. New York: Simon and Schuster, 1950.*

15 *Simple Stakes A Claim*. New York: Rinehart, 1957.*

16 *Simple Takes a Wife*. New York: Simon and Schuster, 1953.*

17 *Simple's Uncle Sam*. New York: Hill and Wang, 1965.*†

18 *Simply Heavenly*. New York: Dramatists Play Service, 1959. (Musical play.

19 *Something in Common and Other Stories*. New York: Hill and Wang, 1963.*†

20 *Tambourines to Glory*. New York: Day, 1958. (Novel.)

21 *The Ways of White Folks*. New York: Knopf, 1934. (Short stories.)*

22 *The Weary Blues*. New York: Knopf, 1926. (Poems.)*

BIBLIOGRAPHIES

23 DICKINSON, Donald C. *A Bio-bibliography of Langston Hughes, 1902–1967*. Hamden, Conn.: Shoe String, 1967.*

24 KAISER, Ernest. "Selected Bibliography of the Published Writings of Langston Hughes." *Freedomways*, VIII (1968), 185–191.

25 O'DANIEL, Therman B. "Langston Hughes: A Selected Classified Bibliography." *CLAJ*, XI (1967), 349–366.

AUTOBIOGRAPHY, BIOGRAPHY, AND CRITICISM

26 See 6.16, 6.17.*

27 ARVEY, Verna. "Langston Hughes: Crusader." *O*, XVIII (1940), 363–64.

28 BONE, Robert. See 31.5.

29 BROWN, Sterling. See 29.21.

1 CLARKE, John H. "Langston Hughes and Jesse B. Semple." *Freedomways*, VIII (1968), 167–169.

2 CULLEN, Countee. "Our Book Shelf: Poet on Poet." *O*, IV (1926),73.*

3 DAVIS, Arthur P. "The Harlem of Langston Hughes' Poetry." *Phylon*, XIII (1952), 276–83.*

4 DAVIS, Arthur P. "Jesse B. Simple: Negro American." *Phylon*, XV (1954), 21–28.*

5 DAVIS, Arthur P. "Langston Hughes: Cool Poet." *CLAJ*, XI (1967), 280–296.

6 DAVIS, Arthur P. "The Tragic Mulatto Theme in Six Works of Langston Hughes." *Phylon*, XVI (1955), 195–204.*

7 EMANUEL, James A. *Langston Hughes*. New York: Twayne, 1967.*

8 EMANUEL, James A. "Langston Hughes' First Short Story: 'Mary Winosky.'" *Phylon*, XXII (1961), 267–73.

9 EMANUEL, James A. "The Literary Experiments of Langston Hughes." *CLAJ*, XI (1967), 335–344.

10 EMANUEL, James A. "The Short Fiction of Langston Hughes." *Freedomways*, VIII (1968), 170–178.

11 EMANUEL, James A. The Short Stories of Langston Hughes. Ph.D. dissertation, Columbia U, 1962.

12 EMBREE, Edwin R. "Langston Hughes: Shakespeare in Harlem." See 10.18.

13 GLOSTER, Hugh M. See 32.3.

14 HUDSON, Theodore R. "Langston Hughes' Last Volume of Verse." *CLAJ*, XI (1967), 345–348. (A review of *The Panther and the Lash*.)

15 HUGHES, Langston. "My Adventures as a Social Poet." *Phylon*, VIII (1947), 205–13.*

16 HUGHES, Langston. "Simple and Me." *Phylon*, VI (1945), 349–54.*

17 ISAACS, Harold. See 24.26.*

18 JACKSON, Blyden. "A Word about Simple." *CLAJ*, XI (1967), 310–318.

19 JONES, Harry L. "A Danish Tribute to Langston Hughes." *CLAJ*, XI (1967), 331–334.

20 LARKIN, Margaret. "A Poet for the People." *O*, V (1927), 84–85.

21 LOCKE, Alain. See 20.14.*

22 MAC LEOD, Norman. "The Poetry and Argument of Langston Hughes." *C*, XLV (1938), 358–59.

23 MARCUS, Steven. See 27.9.

24 MATHEUS, John F. "Langston Hughes as Translator." *CLAJ*, XI (1967), 319–330.

25 MITCHELL, Loften. "For Langston Hughes and Stella Holt: An Informal Memoir." *ND*, XVII (1968), 41–43, 74–77.

26 PETERKIN, Julia. "Negro Blue and Gold." *Poetry*, XXXI (1927), 44–47. (Review of *Fine Clothes to the Jew*.)*

27 PRESLEY, James. "The American Dream of Langston Hughes." *SWR*, XLVIII (1963), 380–86.

28 QUINOT, Raymond. *Langston Hughes, ou l'etoile noire*. Bruxelles: Editions C.E.L.F., 1964.

1 REDDING, Saunders. See 28.13.
2 ROGGE, Heinz. "Die Figur des Simple im Werke von Langston Hughes." *NS*, XII (1955), 555–66.
3 SCHOELL, Frank. "Un poète nègre." *Revue politique et littéraire*, XX (1929), 436–38.
4 SPENCER, T. J. and C. J. RIVERS. "Langston Hughes' Style and Optimism." *Drama Cr*, VII, (Spring, 1964), 99–102.
5 TURNER, Darwin T. "Langston Hughes as Playwright." *CLAJ*, XI (1967), 297–309.
6 WAGNER, Jean. See 34.6.

Hunter, Kristin

7 *God Bless the Child.* New York: Scribner, 1964. (Novel.)

8 *The Landlord.* New York: Scribner, 1966.†

Huntley, Elizabeth Maddox

9 *What Ye Sow.* New York: Court, 1955. (Drama.)

Hurston, Zora Neale

10 *Jonah's Gourd Vine.* Philadelphia: Lippincott, 1934. (Novel.)

11 *Moses, Man of the Mountain.* Philadelphia: Lippincott, 1939. (Novel.)*

12 *Seraph on the Suwanee.* New York: Scribner, 1948. (Novel.)

13 *Their Eyes Were Watching God.* Philadelphia: Lippincott, 1937. (Novel.)*†

AUTOBIOGRAPHY, BIOGRAPHY, AND CRITICISM

14 See 6.18.

15 BONE, Robert. See 31.5.*

16 BYRD, James W. "Zora Neale Hurston: A Novel Folklorist." *TFSB*, XXI (1955), 37–41.

17 GLOSTER, Hugh M. See 32.3.*

18 HUGHES, Langston. See 6.17.*

19 HURST, Fannie. "Zora Hurston: A Personality Sketch." *YULG*, XXXV (1961), 17–22.*

20 JACKSON, Blyden. "Some Negroes in the Land of Goshen." *TFSB*, XIX (1953), 103–7.

21 TURNER, Darwin T. See 33.1.*

Johnson, Fenton

1 *Visions of the Dusk*. New York: The Author, 1915. (Poems.)

2 *Songs of the Soil*. New York: The Author, 1916.

3 *A Little Dreaming*. Chicago: Peterson, 1913. (Poems.)

BIOGRAPHY AND CRITICISM

4 REDDING, Saunders. See 28.13.

Johnson, Georgia Douglas

5 *An Autumn Love Cycle*. New York: Neal, 1938. (Poems.)

6 *Bronze: A Book of Verse*. Boston: Brimmer, 1922.

7 *The Heart of a Woman and Other Poems*. Boston: Cornhill, 1918.

8 *Share My World*. Washington, D.C.: The Author, 1962. (Poems.)

BIOGRAPHY AND CRITICISM

9 BRAWLEY, Benjamin. See 21.21.

10 DOVER, Cedric. "The Importance of Georgia Douglas Johnson." *C*, LIX (1952), 633–36, 674.*

11 REDDING, Saunders. See 28.13.*

Johnson, James Weldon

12 *The Autobiography of an Ex-Coloured Man*. New York: Hill and Wang, 1960. (Novel, originally pub. 1912.)†

13 *Fifty Years and Other Poems*. Boston: Cornhill, 1917.

14 *God's Trombones; Seven Negro Sermons in Verse*. New York: Viking, 1927.

15 *Saint Peter Relates an Incident; Selected Poems*. New York: Viking, 1935.

AUTOBIOGRAPHY, BIOGRAPHY, AND CRITICISM

16 See 6.19.

17 ADELMAN, Lynn. "A Study of James Weldon Johnson." *JNH*, LII (1967), 224–27.

18 APTHEKER, Herbert. "DuBois on James Weldon Johnson." *JNH*, LII (1967), 128–45.

19 AUSLANDER, Joseph. "Sermon Sagas." *O*, V (1927), 274–275. (Review of *God's Trombones*.)*

20 AVERY, William A. "James Weldon Johnson: American Negro of Distinction." *S&S*, XLVIII (1938), 291–94.

1 BAKER, A. "Reading for Democracy: James Weldon Johnson." *WLB*, XVIII (October, 1943), 140–4.

2 BAXTER, Harvey L. "James Weldon Johnson," *C*, XLV (1938), 291.*

3 BONE, Robert. See 31.5.

4 BRAWLEY, Benjamin. See 21.19, 21.21.*

5 BRONZ, Stephen A. See 46.15.*

6 BROWN, Sterling A. See 29.21.*

7 COLLIER, Eugenia W. See 51.5.

8 GLOSTER, Hugh M. See 32.3.

9 POTTS, Eunice B. "James Weldon Johnson: His Legacy to Us." *O*, XVIII (1940), 132–35.

10 REDDING, Saunders. See 28.13.

11 TARRY, Ellen. *Young Jim; the Early Years of James Weldon Johnson.* New York: Dodd, Mead, 1967. (Juvenile.)

12 TATE, E. C. "Sentiment and Horse Sense: James Weldon Johnson's Style." *NHB*, XXV (April, 1962), 152–54.

Jones, LeRoi

13 *The Baptism and the Toilet.* New York: Grove, 1966. (Plays.)†

14 *The Dead Lecturer.* New York: Grove, 1964. (Poems.)*†

15 *Dutchman and the Slave.* New York: Morrow, 1964. (Plays.)†

16 *Preface to a Twenty-Volume Suicide Note.* New York: Corinth, 1961. (Poems.)*

17 *The System of Dante's Hell.* New York: Grove, 1965. (Novel.)†

18 *Tales.* New York: Grove, 1967. (Short stories, essays.)†

BIOGRAPHY AND CRITICISM

19 DENNISON, George. "The Demagogy of LeRoi Jones." *Commentary*, XXXIX (1965), 67–70.

20 FULLER, Hoyt W. See 31.20.*

21 GOTTLIEB, Saul. "They Think You're an Airplane and You're Really a Bird!" *Evergreen Review* No. 50, XI (December, 1967), 50–53, 96–97. (Interview.)

22 HUGHES, Langston. "That Boy LeRoi." *Chicago Defender*, Jan. 11, 1965.

23 LEVERTOV, Denise. "Poets of the Given Ground." *Nation*, CXCII (October 14, 1961), 251–52.

24 LINDENBERG, Daniel. "Un Théâtre militant." *TempsM*, XXI (1966), 1918–20.

25 MAJOR, Clarence. "The Poetry of LeRoi Jones." *ND*, XIV (March, 1965), 54–56.

26 ROTH, Phillip. See 40.4.

1 SMITH, R. H. "Jersey Justice and LeRoi Jones." *PubW*, CXCIII (January 15, 1968), 66.

Kelley, William Melvin

2 *A Different Drummer.* New York: Doubleday, 1962. (Novel.)†

3 *Dancers on the Shore.* Garden City, N.Y.: Doubleday, 1964. (Short stories.)*

4 *Dem.* New York: Doubleday, 1967. (Novel.)

5 *A Drop of Patience.* Garden City, N.Y.: Doubleday, 1965. (Novel.)

BIOGRAPHY AND CRITICISM

6 KELLEY, William M. "If You're Woke You Dig It." *New York Times Magazine* (May 20, 1962), 45.

Killens, John O.

7 *And Then We Heard the Thunder.* New York: Knopf, 1963. (Novel.)†

8 *'Sippi.* New York: Trident, 1967. (Novel.)

9 *Youngblood.* New York: Dial, 1954. (Novel.)

BIOGRAPHY AND CRITICISM

10 MITCHELL, Loften. See 42.7.

Knight, Etheridge

11 *Poems from Prison.* Detroit: Broadside, 1968.

Larsen, Nella

12 *Passing.* New York: Knopf, 1929. (Novel.)

13 *Quicksand.* New York: Knopf, 1928. (Novel.)

BIOGRAPHY AND CRITICISM

14 BONE, Robert. See 31.5.*

15 GLOSTER, Hugh. See 32.3.

16 REDDING, Saunders. See 28.13.*

Lee, Don L.

1 *Black Pride*. Detroit: Broadside, 1968. (Poems.)
2 *Think Black*. Detroit: Broadside, 1968. 2nd rev. ed. (Poems.)

Lee, George W.

3 *Beale Street Sundown*. New York: Field, 1942. (Novel.)
4 *River George*. New York: Macaulay, 1937. (Novel.)

BIOGRAPHY AND CRITICISM

5 BONE, Robert. See 31.5.
6 GLOSTER, Hugh. See 32.3.

Lee, John M.

7 *Counter Clockwise*. New York: Malliet, 1940. (Novel.)

Lorde, Audre

8 *The First Cities*. New York: Poets P, 1967. (Poems.)

Lucas, Curtis

9   *Angel*. New York: Leon, 1943. (Novel.)
10 *Flour Is Dusty*. Philadelphia: Dorrance, 1943. (Novel.)
11 *Forbidden Fruit*. New York: Universal, 1953. (Novel.)
12 *Lila*. New York: Leon, 1955. (Novel.)
13 *So Low, So Lonely*. New York: Leon, 1952. (Novel.)
14 *Third Ward, Newark*. Chicago: Ziff-Davis, 1946. (Novel.)

McGirt, James E.

15 *Avenging the Maine*. Raleigh, N.C.: Edwards & Broughton, 1899. (Poems.)
16 *For Your Sweet Sake*. Philadelphia: Winston, 1906. (Poems.)
17 *Some Simple Songs*. Philadelphia: Larker, 1901. (Poems.)
18 *The Triumphs of Ephraim*. Philadelphia: McGirt, 1907.

BIOGRAPHY AND CRITICISM

1 PARKER, John W. "James E. McGirt: Tarheel Poet." *C*, LX (1953), 286–289.

McKay, Claude

2 *Banana Bottom.* New York: Harper, 1933. (Novel.)*

3 *Banjo.* New York: Harper, 1929. (Novel.)

4 *Gingertown.* New York: Harper, 1932. (Short stories.)

5 *Harlem Shadows.* Introduction by Max Eastman. New York: Harcourt Brace, 1922.

6 *Home to Harlem.* New York: Harper, 1928. (Novel.)*†

7 *Selected Poems.* Introduction by John Dewey and biographical note by Max Eastman. New York: Bookman, 1953.*

8 *Songs of Jamaica.* Kingston, Jamaica, B.W.I.: Gardner, 1912.

9 *Spring in New Hampshire and Other Poems.* London: Richards, 1920.

AUTOBIOGRAPHY, BIOGRAPHY, AND CRITICISM

10 See 7.1.*

11 BONE, Robert A. See 31.5.

12 BRONZ, Stephen A. See 46.15.*

13 BROWN, Sterling A. See 29.21.*

14 BUTCHER, Philip. "Claude McKay—'If We Must Die.'" *O*, XXVI (1948), 127.*

15 COOPER, Wayne. "Claude McKay and the New Negro of the 1920's." *Phylon*, XXV (1964), 297–306.*

16 GLOSTER, Hugh M. See 32.3.

17 JACKSON, Blyden. "The Essential McKay." *Phylon*, XIV (1953), 216–17.

18 LOCKE, Alain. See 20.14.

19 MC KAY, Claude. "Boyhood in Jamaica." *Phylon*, XIV (1953), 134–45.*

20 MC KAY, Claude. "A Negro to His Critics." *New York Herald Tribune Books*, March 6, 1932.

21 REDDING, Saunders. See 28.13.

22 SMITH, Robert A. "Claude McKay: An Essay in Criticism." *Phylon*, IX (1948), 270–73.

MacKey, William W.

23 *Behold! Cometh the Vanderkellans.* New York: Azazel, 1966. (Drama.)

Madden, Will Anthony

1 *Two and One*. New York: Exposition, 1961. (2 stories and drama.)

2 *Five More*. New York: Exposition, 1963. (Short stories.)

Madgett, Naomi Long

3 *One and the Many*. New York: Exposition, 1956. (Poems.)

4 *Star by Star*. Detroit, Mich.: Harlo, 1965. (Poems.)

5 *Songs to a Phantom Nightingale*. New York: Fortuny's, 1941. (Poems.)

Marshall, Paule

6 *Brown Girl, Brownstones*. New York: Random, 1959. (Novel.)*

7 *Soul Clap Hands and Sing*. New York: Atheneum, 1961. (Short stories.)*

Mayfield, Julian

8 *The Grand Parade*. New York: Vanguard, 1961. (Novel.)*† (Appears in paperback edition as *Nowhere Street*.)

9 *The Hit*. New York: Vanguard, 1957. (Novel.)*

10 *The Long Night*. New York: Vanguard, 1958. (Novel.)*

BIOGRAPHY AND CRITICISM

11 FULLER, Hoyt W. See 31.20.

Micheaux, Oscar

12 *The Case of Mrs. Wingate*. New York: Book, 1945.

13 *The Wind from Nowhere*. New York: Book, 1941. (Novel.)

BIOGRAPHY AND CRITICISM

14 BONE, Robert. See 31.5.

Miller, May

1 *Into the Clearing.* Washington, D.C.: Charioteer, 1960.

Mitchell, Loften

2 *A Land Beyond the River.* Cody, Wyoming: Pioneer Drama Service, 1963. (Drama.)

Moreau, Julian

3 *The Black Commandos.* Atlanta, Ga.: Cultural Institute, 1967. (Novel.)

Motley, Willard

4 *Knock at Any Door.* New York: Appleton-Century, 1947.*†
5 *Let No Man Write My Epitaph.* New York: \Random, 1958.
6 *Let Noon Be Fair.* New York: Putnam, 1966.†
7 *Tourist Town.* New York: Putnam, 1965.
8 *We Fished All Night.* New York: Appleton-Century-Crofts, 1951.

BIOGRAPHY AND CRITICISM

9 BONE, Robert A. See 31.5.
10 FORD, Nick A. See 52.19.*
11 "Knock on Any Door." *Look,* XI (Sept. 30, 1947), 21–31.
12 "Willard Motley." *Encyclopedia International.* 2nd ed. New York: Grolier, 1968.*
13 "Willard Motley Dies in Mexico." *New York Times,* March 5, 1965.*

Offord, Carl R.

14 *The Naked Fear.* New York: Ace, 1954. (Novel.)
15 *The White Face.* New York: McBride, 1943. (Novel.)

Ottley, Roi

16 *White Marble Lady.* New York: Farrar, Straus & Giroux, 1965. (Novel.)

Parks, Gordon

1 *The Learning Tree*. New York: Harper & Row, 1963. (Novel.)*†

AUTOBIOGRAPHY

2 *Gordon Parks; A Poet and His Camera*. New York: Viking, 1968. (Poetry.)

Perry, Charles

3 *Portrait of a Young Man Drowning*. New York: Simon and Schuster, 1963. (Novel.)

Peterson, Louis S.

4 *Take a Giant Step*. New York: French, 1954. (Drama.)*

Petry, Ann

5 *Country Place*. Boston: Houghton Mifflin, 1947. (Novel.)
6 *The Narrows*. Boston: Houghton Mifflin, 1953. (Novel.)
7 *The Street*. Boston: Houghton Mifflin, 1946. (Novel.)†
8 *Tituba of Salem Village*. New York: Crowell, 1964. (Fiction for teenagers.)

BIOGRAPHY AND CRITICISM

9 BONE, Robert. See 31.5.*
10 DEMPSEY, Davis. See 83.1.
11 GREEN, Marjorie. "Ann Petry Planned to Write." *O*, XXIV (1946), 78–79.
12 IVY, James. "Ann Petry Talks about First Novel." *C*, LIII (1946), 48–49.
13 IVY, James. "Mrs. Petry's Harlem." *C*, LIII (1946), 43–46.
14 MAUND, Alfred. See 27.12.
15 "On an Author." *New York Herald Tribune*, August 16, 1953.*
16 RICHARDSON, Ben. See 14.10.

Pitcher, Oliver

17 *Dust of Silence*. San Francisco: Troubador, 1960. (*Novel.*)

Polite, Carlene H.

1 *The Flagellants*. New York: Farrar, Straus & Giroux, 1967.†

Randall, Dudley

2 *Cities Burning*. Detroit: Broadside, 1968. (Poems.)

3 (Co-author with Margaret DANNER.) *Poem Counterpoem*. 2nd ed. Detroit: Broadside, 1968.

Redding, Saunders

Mr. Redding has published books under the first names J. Saunders, Jay Saunders and Saunders. For consistency, all publications in this bibliography use Saunders.

4 See 7.3.

5 *Stranger and Alone*. New York: Harcourt, Brace, 1950. (Novel.)

AUTOBIOGRAPHY, BIOGRAPHY, AND CRITICISM

6 See 7.2.

7 BONE, Robert. See 31.5.

Reed, Ishmael

8 *The Free-Lance Pall Bearers: An Irreverent Novel*. Garden City, N.Y.: Doubleday, 1967.

Richardson, Willis

9 See 20.23, 20.24.

10 *The King's Dilemma and Other Plays for Children*. New York: Exposition, 1956.

Rivers, Conrad Kent

11 *The Black Bodies and This Sunburnt Face*. Cleveland: Free Lance, 1963. (Poems.)

Roberson, Sadie

12 *Killer of the Dream*. New York: Carleton, 1963. (Novel.)

Roberts, Walter A.

1 *Brave Mardi Gras.* Indianapolis: Bobbs-Merrill, 1946. (Novel.)

2 *Creole Dusk, a New Orleans Novel of the '80's.* Indianapolis: Bobbs-Merrill, 1948. (Novel.)

3 *The Haunting Hand.* New York: Macaulay, 1926. (Novel.)

4 *Mayor Harding of New York.* New York: Mohawk 1931. (Novel.)

5 *The Moralist.* New York: Mohawk, 1931. (Novel.)

6 *Pierrot Wounded and Other Poems.* New York: Britton, 1919.

7 *The Pomegranate.* Indianapolis: Bobbs-Merrill, 1941. (Novel.)

8 *Royal Street.* Indianapolis: Bobbs-Merrill, 1944. (Novel.)

9 *The Single Star, a Novel of Cuba in the '90's.* Indianapolis: Bobbs-Merrill, 1949.

Rogers, James O.

10 *Blues and Ballads of a Black Yankee.* New York: Exposition, 1965.

Rogers, Joel

11 *She Walks in Beauty.* Los Angeles: Western, 1963. (Novel.)

Savoy, Willard

12 *Alien Land.* New York: Dutton, 1949. (Novel.)

Schuyler, George S.

13 *Black No More.* New York: Macaulay, 1931. (Novel.)

AUTOBIOGRAPHY, BIOGRAPHY, AND CRITICISM

14 See 7.4.

15 BONE, Robert. See 31.5.

16 GLOSTER, Hugh. See 32.3.

Shaw, Letty M.

17 *Angel Mink.* New York: Comet, 1957. (Novel.)

Simmons, Herbert

1 *Corner Boy.* Boston: Houghton Mifflin, 1957. (Novel.)†
2 *Man Walking on Eggshells.* Boston: Houghton Mifflin, 1962. (Novel.)

Smith, William Gardner

3 *Anger at Innocence.* New York: Farrar, Straus, 1950. (Novel.)
4 *South Street.* New York: Farrar, Straus, 1954. (Novel.)
5 *The Last of the Conquerors.* New York: Farrar, Straus, 1948. (Novel.)*†
6 *The Stone Face.* New York: Farrar, Straus, 1963. (Novel.)*

BIOGRAPHY AND CRITICISM

7 BONE, Robert S. See 31.5.

Spellman, A. B.

8 *The Beautiful Days.* New York: Poet's P, 1965. (Poems.)

Stevens, Shane

9 *Go Down Dead.* New York: Morrow, 1967. (Novel.)†

Thomas, Will

10 *God is for White Folks.* New York: Creative Age, 1947. (Novel.)
11 *The Seeking.* New York: Wyn, 1953. (Novel.)

Thurman, Wallace

12 *The Blacker the Berry.* New York: Macaulay, 1929. (Novel.)*
13 *Infants of the Spring.* New York: Macaulay, 1932.*

BIOGRAPHY AND CRITICISM

14 BONE, Robert. See 31.5.*
15 GLOSTER, Hugh. See 32.3.*
16 HUGHES, Langston. See 24.19.*

Tolson, Melvin B.

1   *Harlem Gallery, Book I: The Curator.* New York: Twayne, 1965. (Poems.)*

2   *Libretto for the Republic of Liberia.* New York: Twayne, 1953.*

3   *Rendezvous with America.* New York: Dodd, Mead, 1944.

BIOGRAPHY AND CRITICISM

4   FABIO, Sarah Webster. "Who Speaks Negro?" *ND*, XVI (December, 1966), 54–58.

5   MC CALL, Dan. "The Quicksilver Sparrow of M. B. Tolson." *AQ*, XVIII (1966), 538–42.

6   RANDALL, Dudley. "Melvin B. Tolson: Portrait of a Poet as Raconteur." *ND*, XV (January, 1966), 54–57.

7   SHAPIRO, Karl. "Melvin B. Tolson, Poet." *Book Week, New York Herald Tribune*, January 10, 1965. Reprinted in *ND*, XIV (May, 1965), 75–77.

8   TATE, Allen. "Preface to *Libretto for the Republic of Liberia.*" *Poetry* LXXVI (1950), 216–18.

9   THOMPSON, D. G. "Tolson's Gallery Brings Poetry Home." *NHB*, XXIX (1965), 69–70.

10 TOLSON, Melvin B. "A Poet's Odyssey." See 24.14, pp. 181–203. (An interview.)

Toomer, Jean

11 *Cane.* New York: Boni & Liveright, 1923. (Poetry, short stories, and sketches; reprinted by University Place P, 1967; Harper, 1968.†)*

12 *Essentials: Definitions and Aphorisms.* Chicago: Lakeside, 1931.

BIOGRAPHY AND CRITICISM

13 BONE, Robert. See 31.5.

14 BONTEMPS, Arna. "The Harlem Renaissance." *SR*, XXX (March 22, 1947), 12–13, 44.

15 BONTEMPS, Arna. "The Negro Renaissance: Jean Toomer and the Harlem Writers of the 1920's." See 24.14, pp. 20–36.*

16 DUBOIS, W. E. B. and Alain LOCKE. "The Younger Literary Movement." *Crisis*, XXVII (1924), 161–63.

17 FULLINWIDER, S. P. "Jean Toomer, Lost Generation, or Negro Renaissance?" *Phylon*, XXVII (1966), 396–403.

18 GLOSTER, Hugh M. See 32.3.

19 HOLMES, Eugene. "Jean Toomer, Apostle of Beauty." *O*, III (1925), 252–54, 260.

20 LOCKE, Alain. See 20.14, 26.17.*

21 MUNSON, Gorham. "The Significance of Jean Toomer." *O*, III (1925), 262–63.*

22 REDDING, Saunders. See 28.13.*

1 ROSENFELD, Paul. "Jean Toomer." *Men Seen*. New York: Dial, 1925.

2 TURNER, Darwin T. "And Another Passing." *NALF*, (Fall, 1967), 3–4.

3 TURNER, Darwin T. "Jean Toomer's *Cane*." *ND*, XVIII (January, 1969), 54–61.

4 TURNER, Darwin T. "The Failure of a Playwright." *CLAJ*, X (1966), 308–318.

Turner, Darwin T.

5 *Katharsis*. Wellesley, Mass.: Wellesley P, 1964. (Poems.)

Turpin, Waters Edward

6 *O Canaan; a Novel*. New York: Doubleday, Doran, 1939.

7 *The Rootless*. New York: Vantage, 1957. (Novel.)

8 *These Low Grounds*. New York: Harper, 1937. (Novel.)*

BIOGRAPHY AND CRITICISM

9 BONE, Robert. See 31.5.

10 GLOSTER, Hugh. See 32.3.

Van Dyke, Henry

11 *Ladies of the Rachmaninoff Eyes*. New York: Farrar, Straus & Giroux, 1965. (Novel.)*

Van Peebles, Melvin

12 *A Bear for the F.B.I.* New York: Trident P, 1968. (Novel.)

Vroman, Mary Elizabeth

13 *Esther*. New York: Bantam, 1963. (Novel.)†

14 *Harlem Summer*. New York: Berkeley, 1968. (Novel.)†

Walker, Margaret

15 *For My People*. New Haven, Conn.: Yale UP, 1942. (Poems.)*†

16 *Jubilee*. Boston: Houghton Mifflin, 1966. (Novel.)*†

BIOGRAPHY AND CRITICISM

(Only book reviews, which can be located through *Book Review Digest*.)

Walrond, Eric
(Born in West Indies, but identified with Harlem Renaissance.)

1 *Tropic Death*. New York: Boni & Liveright, 1926. (Short stories.)

Ward, Douglas T.

2 *Happy Ending* and *Day of Absence*. New York: Dramatists Play Service, 1968.

Webb, Frank J.

3 *The Garies and Their Friends*. London: Routledge, 1857. (Novel.)

BIOGRAPHY AND CRITICISM

4 GLOSTER, Hugh. See 32.3.

West, Dorothy

5 *The Living Is Easy*. Boston: Houghton Mifflin, 1948. (Novel.)

BIOGRAPHY AND CRITICISM

6 BONE, Robert. See 31.5.

West, John

7   *Bullets Are My Business*. New York: New American Library, 1960. (Novel.)
8   *Cobra Venom*. New York: New American Library, 1959. (Novel.)
9   *Death on the Rocks*. New York: New American Library, 1961. (Novel.)†
10 *An Eye for an Eye*. New York: New American Library, 1959. (Novel.)
11 *A Taste for Blood*. New York: New American Library, 1960. (Novel.)

Wheatley, Phillis

12 HEARTMAN, Charles F., ed. *Phillis Wheatley (Phillis Peters): Poems and Letters*. New York: The Author, n.d.

13 MASON, Julian, ed. *The Poems of Phillis Wheatley*. Chapel Hill: U of North Carolina P, 1966.*

14 *Memoir and Poems of Phillis Wheatley; also Poems by a Slave*. 3rd ed. Boston: Knapp, 1838.

BIOGRAPHY AND CRITICISM

15 BRAWLEY, Benjamin. See 21.19.

1   DAVIS, Arthur. "Personal Elements in the Poetry of Phillis Wheatley." *Phylon*, XIV (1953), 191–98.*

2   GRAHAM, Shirley. *The Story of Phillis Wheatley: Poetess of the American Revolution.* New York: Messner, 1949.

3   GREGORY, Montgomery. "The Spirit of Phillis Wheatley." *O*, I (1923), 374–75.

4   HEARTMAN, Charles F. *Phillis Wheatley (Phillis Peters): A Critical Attempt and a Bibliography of Her Writings.* New York: The Author, 1915.

5   HOLMES, Welfred. "Phillis Wheatley." *NHB*, VI (1943), 117–18.*

6   LOGGINS, Vernon. See 27.8.*

7   MASON, Julian. "Introduction." See 75.13.*

8   MATTHEWS, A. "The Writings of Phillis Wheatley." *N&Q*, CLIX (July 12, 1930), 30–31.

9   QUARLES, Benjamin A. "Documents." *JNH*, XXXIV (1949), 462–64. (A Phillis Wheatley letter.)

10   REDDING, Saunders. See 28.13.

11   RENFRO, Herbert G., ed. *Life and Works of Phillis Wheatley.* Washington, D.C.: Pendleton, 1916.

12   SLATTERY, J. R. "Phillis Wheatley, the Negro Poetess." *CathW*, XXXIX (1884), 483–98.

White, Walter

13   *The Fire in the Flint.* New York: Knopf, 1924. (Novel.)

14   *Flight.* New York: Knopf, 1926. (Novel.)

BIOGRAPHY AND CRITICISM

15   BONE, Robert. See 31.5.

16   GLOSTER, Hugh. See 32.3.

Whitman, Albery Allson

17   *An Idyl of the South: An Epic Poem in Two Parts.* New York: Metaphysical, 1901.

18   *Not a Man, and Yet a Man.* Springfield, Ohio: Republic, 1877. (Poems.)

19   *The Rape of Florida.* 3rd ed. St. Louis: Nixon-Jones, 1890. (Poetry.)

BIOGRAPHY AND CRITICISM

20   LOGGINS, Vernon. See 27.8.*

21   REDDING, Saunders. See 28.13.*

Wideman, John Edgar

1   *A Glance Away*. New York: Harcourt, Brace & World, 1967. (Novel.)

Williams, Chancellor

2   *Have You Been to the River?* New York: Exposition, 1952.
3   *The Raven*. Philadelphia: Dorrance, 1943.

Williams, John A.

4   *The Angry Ones*. New York: Ace, 1960. (Novel.)
5   *The Man Who Cried I Am*. Boston: Little, Brown, 1967. (Novel.)*
6   *Night Song*. New York: Farrar, Straus, 1961. (Novel.)*
7   *Sissie*. New York: Farrar, Straus, 1963. (Novel.)*

BIOGRAPHY AND CRITICISM

8   FULLER, Hoyt W. See 31.20.*
9   LEE, Don L. "*The Man Who Cried I Am*." *ND*, XVII (March, 1968), 51–52, 77–79.

Wright, Charles

10 *The Messenger*. New York: Farrar, Straus, 1963. (Novel.)
11 *The Wig*. New York: Farrar, Straus & Giroux, 1966. (Novel.)

Wright, Richard

12 See 7.8.
13 *Eight Men*. New York: World, 1961. (Short stories.)*†
14 *Lawd, Today*. New York: Avon, 1963. (Novel.)†
15 *The Long Dream*. Garden City, N.Y.: Doubleday, 1958. (Novel.)*
16 *Native Son*. New York: Harper, 1940. (Novel.)*†
17 *The Outsider*. New York: Harper, 1953. (Novel.)*†
18 *Savage Holiday*. New York: Universal, 1965. (Novel.)†
19 *Uncle Tom's Children*. New York: Harper, 1947. (Orig. pub. 1938.) (Short stories.)*†

BIBLIOGRAPHY

20 BRYER, Jackson R. "Richard Wright: A Selected Check List of Criticism." *WSCL*, I (1960), 22–33.*

1 FABRE, Michel, and Edward MARGOLIES. "Richard Wright (1908–1960)." *BB*, XXIV (1965), 131–33, 137. (Also in 80.2.) (Works about Richard Wright.)*

2 SPRAGUE, M. D. "Richard Wright: A Bibliography." *BB*, XXI (1953), 39. (Works by Richard Wright.)*

AUTOBIOGRAPHY, BIOGRAPHY, AND CRITICISM

3 See 7.7.

4 BALDWIN, James. "Alas Poor Richard." *Nobody Knows My Name*. New York: Dial, 1961.

5 BALDWIN, James. "Ce qui survivra de Richard Wright." *Preuves*, No. 16 (1963), 76–79.*

6 BALDWIN, James. "Everybody's Protest Novel." *PR*, XVI (1949), 578–85. (Reprinted in 6.5.)*

7 BALDWIN, James. "Many Thousands Gone." *Notes of a Native Son*. Boston: Beacon, 1955.

8 BALDWIN, James. "Richard Wright." *Encounter*, XVI, (1961), 58–60.*

9 BALDWIN, James. "Survival of Richard Wright." *Reporter*, XXIV (March 15, 1961), 24.

10 BISOL, Gaetano. "Richard Wright: Drama razziale e narrative negra di protesta." *Letture*, XX (1965), 259–76.

11 "Black Boy." *Life*, XVIII (June 3, 1945), 87–93.

12 BONE, Robert. See 31.5.

13 BURGUM, Edwin B. "The Promise of Democracy in Richard Wright's *Native Son*." *The Novel and the World's Dilemma*. New York: Oxford UP, 1947.

14 CHARNEY, Maurice. See 38.6.*

15 COHN, David L. "The Negro Novel: Richard Wright." *AtM*, CLXV (1940), 659–61.

16 CREEKMORE, Hubert. "Social Factors in Native Son." *UKCR*, VIII (1941), 136–43.

17 DAVIS, Arthur P. "*The Outsider* as a Novel of Race." *MJ*, VII (1955–56), 320–26.*

18 ELLISON, Ralph. "Richard Wright's Blues." *AR*, V (1945), 198–211. (Reprinted in 6.14.)*

19 EMBREE, Edwin. "Richard Wright, Native Son." See 10.18.

20 FLEURENT, Maurice. "Richard Wright a Paris." *Paru*, No. 25, December, 1946, 7–8.

21 FONTAINE, William T. See 23.14.*

22 FORD, Nick A. "The Ordeal of Richard Wright." *CE*, XV (1953), 87–94.

23 FORD, Nick A. "Richard Wright, a Profile." *CJF*, XXI (1962), 26–30.*

1 FULLER, Hoyt W. See 31.20.

2 GÉRARD, Albert. See 31.21.

3 GÉRARD, Albert. "Vie et vocation de Richard Wright." *RGB*, XCVII (1961), 65–78.

4 GLICKSBERG, Charles I. "Existentialism in *The Outsider*." *Four Quarters*, VII (1958), 17–26.

5 GLOSTER, Hugh. See 32.3.

6 GLOSTER, Hugh M. "Richard Wright: Interpreter of Racial and Economic Maladjustments." XIX (1941), 361–65.

7 HARRINGTON, Ollie. "The Last Days of Richard Wright." *Ebony*, XVI (February, 1961), 83–6.*

8 HILL, Herbert *et al.* "Reflections on Richard Wright: A Symposium on an Exiled Native Son." See 24.14, pp. 196–212.*

9 HOWE, Irving. "Black Boys and Native Sons." *A World More Attractive*. New York: Horizon, 1963.*

10 HOWE, Irving. "Richard Wright: A Word of Farewell." *NR*, CXLIV (February 13, 1961), 17–18.

11 ISAACS, Harold. See 24.26.

12 JACKSON, Esther. See 25.8.

13 JONES, Howard M. "Up from Slavery: Richard Wright's Story." *SatR*, XXVIII (March 3, 1945), 9–10.

14 KNOX, George. See 32.17.

15 LEWIS, T. "Saga of Bigger Thomas." *CathW*, CLIII (1941), 201–06.

16 LOCKE, Alain. See 26.17.

17 MARCUS, Steven. See 27.9.

18 MARGOLIES, Edward L. *The Art of Richard Wright*. Carbondale, Ill.: Southern Illinois UP, 1969. See also 27.10.

19 MAUND, Alfred. See 27.12.

20 MC CALL, Dan. *The Example of Richard Wright*. New York: Harcourt, Brace and World, 1969.

21 MURRAY, Albert. See 32.23.

22 RASCOE, Burton. "Negro Novel and White Reviewers." *AMer*, L (1940), 113–17. (*Native Son*.)

23 REDDING, Saunders. "The Alien Land of Richard Wright." See 20.1, pp. 48–59.

24 REDDING, Saunders. "Home Is Where the Heart Is." *NL* (December 11, 1961), 24–25.

25 ROGGE, Heinz. See 53.18.

26 SCOTT, Nathan A., Jr. "The Dark and Haunted Tower of Richard Wright." *Graduate Comment*, VII (1964), 92–99.

27 SCOTT, Nathan A. "A Search for Beliefs: The Fiction of Richard Wright." *UKCR*, XXIII (1956), 19–24, 130–38.*

28 SILLEN, Samuel. "The Meaning of Bigger Thomas." *New Masses*, XXXV (1960), 13–21.

29 TURNER, Darwin T. "The Outsider: Revision of an Idea." *CLAJ*, XII (1968), 310–321.

1   TURNER, Darwin T. See 33.1.

2   WEBB, Constance. *Richard Wright, a Biography*. New York: Putnam, 1968.

3   WEBB, Constance. "What Next for Richard Wright?" *Phylon*, X (1949), 161–67.

4   WHITE, Ralph K. "Black Boy: A Valuable Analysis." *JASP*, XLII (1947), 440–61.

5   WIDMER, Kingsley. "The Existential Darkness: Richard Wright's *The Outsider*." *WSCL*, I (1960), 13–21.*

6   WILLIAMS, John A. "Introduction." See 7.8.

7   WINSLOW, Henry F. "Richard Nathaniel Wright: Destroyer and Preserver (1908–1960)." *C*, LXIX (1962), 149–63, 187.*

8   WRIGHT, Richard. "Early Days in Chicago." *Cross Section*. Ed. Edwin Seaver. New York: Fischer, 1945.

9   WRIGHT, Richard. "How Bigger Was Born." *SatR*, XXII (June 1, 1940), 3–4.*

10   WRIGHT, Richard. "Richard Wright." *The God That Failed*. Ed. Richard Crossman. New York: Harper & Row, 1950.†

Yerby, Frank

11   *Benton's Row*. New York: Dial, 1954. (Novel.)

12   *Bride of Liberty*. New York: Doubleday, 1954. (Novel for teenagers.)

13   *Captain Rebel*. New York: Dial, 1956. (Novel.)*†

14   *The Devil's Laughter*. New York: Dial, 1953. (Novel.)†

15   *Fairoaks*. New York: Dial, 1957. (Novel.)†

16   *Floodtide*. New York: Dial, 1950. (Novel.)†

17   *The Foxes of Harrow*. New York: Dial, 1946. (Novel.)*†

18   *The Garfield Honor*. New York: Dial, 1961. (Novel.)†

19   *Gillian*. New York: Dial, 1960. (Novel.)†

20   *Goat Song*. New York: Dial, 1967. (Novel.)

21   *The Golden Hawk*. New York: Dial, 1948. (Novel.)†

22   *Griffin's Way*. New York: Dial, 1962. (Novel.)†

23   *Jarrett's Jade*. New York: Dial, 1959. (Novel.)†

24   *An Odor of Sanctity*. New York: Dial, 1965. (Novel.)*†

25   *The Old Gods Laugh*. New York: Dial, 1964. (Novel.)†

26   *Pride's Castle*. New York: Dial, 1949. (Novel.)*†

27   *The Saracen Blade*. New York: Dial, 1952. (Novel.)*†

28   *The Serpent and the Staff*. New York: Dial, 1958. (Novel.)†

29   *The Treasure of Pleasant Valley*. New York: Dial, 1955. (Novel.)

30   *The Vixens*. New York: Dial, 1947. (Novel.)†

31   *A Woman Called Fancy*. New York: Dial, 1951. (Novel.)†

BIOGRAPHY AND CRITICISM

1 FORD, Nick A. See 52.19.*

2 FULLER, Hoyt W. "Famous Writer Faces a Challenge." *Ebony*, XXI (June, 1966), 188–90, 192–94.*

3 GLOSTER, Hugh. "The Significance of Frank Yerby." *C*, LV (1948), 12–14.*

4 "The Golden Corn: He Writes to Please." *Time*, LV (November 29, 1954), 97.

5 "Mystery Man of Letters." *Ebony*, X (February, 1955), 31–32, 35–38.

6 TURNER, Darwin T. See 33.1.

7 TURNER, Darwin T. "Frank Yerby as Debunker." *MR*, IX (1968), 569–577.*

8 YERBY, Frank. "How and Why I Write the Costume Novel." *Harpers*, CCXIV (October, 1959), 145–50.*

Appendix: Selected Criticism of Africans and Afro-Americans as Characters

9 ALTENBERND, Lynn. "Huck Finn, Emancipator." *Criticism*, I (1959), 298–307.

10 AMACHER, Anne Ward. "The General Primitivist and the Semi-tragic Octoroon." *NEQ*, XXIX (1956), 216–27.

11 BACKMAN, Melvin. "The Wilderness and the Negro in Faulkner's *The Bear*." *PMLA*, LXXVI (1961), 595–600.

12 BECK, Warren. "Faulkner and the South." *AR*, I (1941), 82–94.

13 BEJA, Morris. "It Must Be Important: The Negro in Contemporary American Fiction." *AR*, XXIV (1964), 323–36.*

14 BLOOMFIELD, Maxwell. "Dixon's *The Leopard's Spots*: A Study in Popular Racism." *AQ*, XVI (1964), 387–401.

15 BRADFORD, Melvin E. "Brotherhood in 'The Bear': An Exemplum for Critics." *ModA*, X (1966), 278–81.

16 BRAVERMAN, Howard. "An Unusual Characterization by a Southern Ante-Bellum Writer." *Phylon*, XIX (1958), 171–79.

17 BRAWLEY, Benjamin. See 31.6.

18 BRICKELL, H. "The Negro as Hero." *PubW*, CXVIII (1930), 583–5.

19 BROWN, Sterling A. "The American Race Problem as Reflected in American Literature." *JNE*, VIII (1939), 275–90.*

20 BROWN, Sterling A. "A Century of Negro Portraiture in American Literature." *MR*, VII (1966), 73–96.*

21 BROWN, Sterling A. "Negro Character as Seen by White Authors." *JNE*, II (1933), 179–203.*

22 BROWN, Sterling A. See 29.21, 31.7.

1 BROWNELL, Francis V. "The Role of Jim in *Huckleberry Finn*." *BosUs*, I (1955), 74–83.

2 BROOKS, Van Wyck. "Eugene O'Neill: Harlem." *The Confident Years: 1885–1915*. New York: Dutton, 1927.

3 BULLOCK, Penelope. "The Mulatto in American Fiction." *Phylon*, VI (1945), 78–82.

4 BURCH, Charles E. "Negro Characters in the Novels of William Gilmore Simms." *SoW*, LII (1923), 192–95.

5 BUTCHER, Philip. *George Washington Cable*. New York: Twayne, 1962.*†

6 BUTCHER, Philip. "Mark Twain Sells Roxy Down the River." *CLAJ*, VIII (1965), 225–33.*

7 CAMPBELL, Killis. "Poe's Treatment of the Negro and Negro Dialect." *UTSE*, XVI (1936), 107–14.

8 CANTOR, Milton. "The Image of the Negro in Colonial Literature." *NEQ*, XXXVI (1963), 452–77.

9 CARTER, Everett. "Cultural History Written with Lightning: The Significance of *The Birth of a Nation*." *AQ*, XII (1960), 347–57.

10 CHADWICK, Hansen. "The Character of Jim and the Ending of *Huckleberry Finn*." *MR*, V (1965), 45–66.

11 CISMARU, A. "The American Negro in Post-War French Drama." *NHB*, XXVII (1964), 79–80.

12 CLARK, Leadie M. *Walt Whitman's Concept of the American Common Man*. New York: Philosophical Library, 1955.

13 CLARKE, John H., ed. *William Styron's Nat Turner: Ten Black Writers Respond*. Boston: Beacon, 1968.

14 CLAY, Eugene. "The Negro in Recent American Literature." *American Writers' Congress*. New York, 1935.

15 CLINE, J. "Rise of the American Stage Negro." *Drama*, XXI (January, 1931), 9–10.

16 COTTON, L. J. "The Negro in the American Theatre." *NHB*, XXIII (1960), 172–78.

17 COUCH, William, Jr. "The Problem of Negro Character and Dramatic Incident." *Phylon*, XI (1950), 127–33.*

18 COX, James. "Pudd'nhead Wilson: The End of Mark Twain's American Dream." *SAQ*, LVIII (1959), 351–63.

19 CRIPPS, Thomas R. See 16.12.

20 DAMON, S. Foster. "The Negro in Early American Songsters." *PBSA*, XXVIII (1934), 132–63.

21 DA PONTE, Durant. "The Greatest Play of the South." *TSL*, II (1957), 15–24. (*The Clansman*.)

22 DAYKIN, Walter I. "Negro Types in American White Fiction." *S&SR*, XXII (1937), 45–52.

23 D'AZEVEDO, Warren. "Revolt on the San Dominick." *Phylon*, XVII (1956), 129–40.

1 DEMPSEY, David. "Uncle Tom's Ghost and the Literary Abolitionist." *AR*, VI (1946), 442–48.*

2 DOHERTY, Herbert J. "Voices of Protest from the New South." *MVHR*, XLII (1955), 45–66.

3 DOWNS, Robert B. *Books That Changed the World*. Chicago: American Library Association, 1956. (*Uncle Tom's Cabin*.)†

4 DRAKE, B. M. *The Negro in Southern Literature Since the War*. Nashville Tenn.: Presbyterian, 1898.

5 DUFNER, Angeline. "The Negro in the American Novel." *ABR*, XVIII (1967), 122–46.

6 DUMBLE, W. R. "A Footnote to Negro Literature." *NHB*, IX (1946), 82–84.

7 DURHAM, Frank M. *DuBose Heyward, The Man Who Wrote Porgy*. Columbia: U of South Carolina P, 1954.

8 DUVALL, Severn. "*Uncle Tom's Cabin:* The Sinister Side of the Patriarchy." *NEQ*, XXXVI (1963), 3–22.

9 EDMONDS, Irene C. "Faulkner and the Black Shadow." *Southern Renascence*. Ed. Louis D. Rubin and Robert D. Jacobs. Baltimore: Johns Hopkins P, 1953, pp. 192–206.

10 EGAN, L. H. "Future of the Negro in Fiction." *Dial*, XVIII (February 1, 1895), 70.

11 ELLISON, Ralph. "Twentieth Century Fiction and the Black Mask of Humanity." See 6.14.*

12 FAULKNER, Seldon. "*The Octoroon* War." *ETJ*, XV (1963), 33–38.

13 FIEDLER, Leslie. "'Come Back to the Raft Ag'in Huck Honey!'" *PR*, XV (1948), 664–71. Reprinted in *An End to Innocence*. Boston: Beacon, 1955.

14 FORD, Nick Aaron. "How Genuine Is *The Green Pastures*?" *Phylon*, XX (1959), 67–70.

15 FORD, Thomas W. "The Miscegenation Theme in *Pudd'nhead Wilson*." *MTJ*, X (1955), 13–14.

16 FORREY, Robert. "Herman Melville and the Negro Question." *Mainstream*, XV (February, 1962), 28–29.

17 GAINES, Francis P. "The Racial Bar Sinister in American Romance." *SAQ*, XXV (1926), 396–402.

18 GAREY, Doris B. "*The Green Pastures* Again." *Phylon*, XX (1959), 193–94.

19 GEISMAR, Maxwell. "William Faulkner: The Negro and the Female." *Writers in Crisis*. Boston: Houghton Mifflin, 1942.

20 GÉRARD, Albert. "William Faulkner, ou le fardeau de l'homme noir." *La Revue nouvelle*, XXIV (1956), 331–38.

21 GLICKSBERG, Charles I. "William Faulkner and the Negro Problem." *Phylon*, X (1949), 153–60.

22 GLICKSBERG, Charles I. "Melville and the Negro Problem." *Phylon*, XI (1950), 207–15.

23 GLICKSBERG, Charles I. "Walt Whitman and the Negro." *Phylon*, IX (1948), 326–31.

1 GLOSTER, Hugh M. "Southern Justice." *Phylon*, X (1949), 93–95.

2 GOLDMAN, Hannah S. "The Tragic Gift: The Serf and Slave Intellectual in Russian and American Fiction." *Phylon*, XXIV (1963), 51–62.

3 GREEN, Elizabeth Lay. See 1.11.

4 GREER, Dorothy. "Dilsey and Lucas: Faulkner's Use of the Negro as Gauge of Moral Character." *ESRS*, XII (1962), 43–61.

5 GROSS, Theodore. *Albion W. Tourgée.* New York: Twayne, 1963.†

6 GROSS, Theodore. "The Fool's Errand of Albion W. Tourgée." *Phylon*, XXIV (1963), 240–54.

7 GROSS, Theodore. "The Negro in the Literature of Reconstruction." *Phylon*, XXII (1961), 5–14.

8 GUTTMAN, Allen. "The Enduring Innocence of Captain Amasa Delano." *BosUs*, V (1961), 35–45.

9 HALPER, Albert. "Whites Writing Up the Blacks." *Dial*, LXXXVI (1929), 29–30.

10 HAMBLEN, Abigail. "Uncle Tom and 'Nigger Jim': A Study in Contrasts and Similarities." *MTJ*, XI, iii (1961) 13–17.

11 HOWE, Irving. "William Faulkner and the Negroes: A Vision of Lost Fraternity." *Commentary*, XII (1951), 359–68.

12 HOWE, Russell Warren. "Prejudice, Superstition, and Economics." *Phylon*, XVII (1956), 215–22.

13 HOWELL, Elmo. "A Note on Faulkner's Negro Characters." *MissQ*, XI (1958), 201–03.

14 HUDSON, Benjamin F. "Another View of 'Uncle Tom'." *Phylon*, XXIV (1963), 79–87.

15 ISAACS, Neil D. "Life for Phoenix." *SR*, LXXI (1963), 75–81.

16 JACKSON, Esther. See 25.8.*

17 JACKSON, Margaret Y. "Melville's Use of a Real Slave Mutiny in *Benito Cereno.*" *CLAJ*, IV (1960), 79–93.

18 JARRETT, Thomas. "Stribling's Novels." *Phylon*, IV (1943), 345–50.

19 JAYNES, Bryson L. "Artemus Ward on the Negro." *RS*, XXXIII (1965), 178–80.

20 JONES, Iva G. "Trollope, Carlyle, and Mill on the Negro: An Episode in the History of Ideas." *JNH*, LII (1967), 185–99.

21 KAISER, Ernest. "Literature on the South." *Freedomways*, IV (1964), 149–67.

22 KALUS, Rosemarie. "Mark Twain und die Negerfrage—*Huckleberry Finn.*" *ZAA*, V (1957), 166–81.

23 KAPLAN, Sidney. "Herman Melville and the American National Sin: The Meaning of *Benito Cereno.*" *JNH*, XLI (1956), 311–38; XLII (1957), 11–37.

24 KAPLAN, Sidney, ed. "Introduction." *The Narrative of Arthur Gordon Pym.* New York: Hill and Wang, 1960.

25 KAPLAN, Sidney. "*The Octoroon:* Early History of the Drama of Miscegenation." *JNE*, XX (1951), 547–57.

26 KAZIN, Alfred. "The Stillness of 'Light in August'." *PR*, XXIV (1957), 519–38.

1 LAW, Robert A. "Mrs. Peterkin's Negroes." *SWR*, XIV (1929), 455–61.

2 LEE, Wallace *et al.* "Is *Uncle Tom's Cabin* Anti-Negro?" *ND*, IV (January, 1946), 68–72.

3 LEVIN, Harry. "Journey to the End of Night." *The Power of Blackness.* New York: Knopf, 1958.

4 LIVELY, Robert A. *Fiction Fights the Civil War.* Chapel Hill: U of North Carolina P, 1957.

5 LOGAN, Rayford W. "The Negro as Portrayed in the Leading Literary Magazines." See 13.1.

6 LOWELL, J. "Eugene O'Neill's Darker Brother." *ThA*, XXXII (1948), 45–58.

7 LUEDERS, Edward G. *Carl Van Vechten.* Albuquerque: U of New Mexico P, 1955.†

8 MAC TAVISH, N. "Original Uncle Tom." *CM*, XXX (November, 1907), 25–9.

9 MC CULLOUGH, Norman V. *The Negro in English Literature.* Devon, Eng.: Stockwell, 1962.

10 MC DOWELL, Tremaine. "Notes on Negro Dialect in the American Novel to 1821." *ASp*, V (1930), 291–96.

11 MC DOWELL, Tremaine. "The Negro in the Southern Novel Prior to 1850." *JEGP*, XXV (1926), 455–73.

12 MARLEY, Harold. "The Negro in Recent Southern Literature." *SAQ*, XXVII (1928), 29–41.

13 MARX, Leo. "Mr. Eliot, Mr. Trilling, and *Huckleberry Finn*." *AmS*, XXII (1953), 423–40.

14 MORRIS, J. A. "Gullah in the Stories and Novels of William Gilmore Simms." *ASp*, XXII (1947), 46–53.

15 "The Negro in Art: How Shall He Be Portrayed?" *C*, XXXI (1926), 219–20, 278–80; XXXII (1926), 35–36, 71–73. (A symposium.)

16 NICHOLAS, Herbert G. "*Uncle Tom's Cabin*, 1852–1952." *GaR*, VIII (1954), 140–48.

17 NICHOLS, Charles. "The Origins of *Uncle Tom's Cabin*." *Phylon*, XIX (1958), 328–34.

18 NILON, Charles. *Faulkner and The Negro.* New York: Citadel, 1965.†

19 NOCK, S. A. "The Essential Farce." *Phylon*, XX (1959), 358–63.

20 NOLEN, W. "The Colored Child in Contemporary Literature." *Horn Book*, XVIII (1942), 348–55.

21 O'DANIEL, Therman B. "Cooper's Treatment of the Negro." *Phylon*, VIII (1947), 164–75.

22 OLIVER, Egbert S. "The Little Cabin of Uncle Tom." *CE*, XXVI (1964), 355–61.

23 OLSEN, Otto H. See 13.16.

24 OSOFSKY, Gilbert. "Symbols of the Jazz Age: the New Negro and Harlem Discovered." *AQ*, XVII (1965), 229–36.

25 OVERSTREET, Harry A. "Images and the Negro." *SatR*, XXVII (August 26, 1944), 5–6.

1 PATTERSON, Cecil L. "A Different Drum: The Image of the Negro in the Nineteenth Century Songster." *CLAJ*, VIII (1964), 44–50.

2 PEDERSON, Lee. "Negro Speech in *The Adventures of Huckleberry Finn*." *MTJ*, XIII, i (1966), 1–4.

3 QUINN, Arthur Hobson. "Literature, Politics, and Slavery." *The Literature of the American People.* Ed. A. H. Quinn. New York: Appleton-Century-Crofts, 1951.

4 REMES, Carol. "The Heart of *Huckleberry Finn*." *M&M*, VIII (November, 1955), 8–16.

5 RIDGELEY, Joseph. "*Woodcraft:* Simms' First Answer to *Uncle Tom's Cabin*." *AL*, XXXI (1960), 421–33.

6 ROLLINS, Hyder E. "The Negro in the Southern Short Story." *SR*, XXIV (1916), 42–60.

7 ROPPOLO, Joseph P. "Uncle Tom in New Orleans: Three Lost Plays." *NEQ*, XXVII (1954), 213–26.

8 SAKAE, Morioka. "*Pudd'nhead Wilson* and the Racial Problem." *SELL* (Fukuoka, Japan), No. 12 (1962), 1–11.

9 SCHIFFMAN, Joseph. "Critical Problems in Melville's *Benito Cereno*." *MLQ*, XI (1950), 317–24.

10 SEIDEN, Melvin. "Faulkner's Ambiguous Negro." *MR*, IV (1963), 675–90.

11 SHELTON, Austin J. "African Realistic Commentary on Culture Hierarchy and Racistic Sentimentalism in *The Yemasee*." *Phylon*, XXV (1964), 72–78.

12 SIMBOLI, David. "'Benito Cereno' as Pedagogy." *CLAJ*, IX (1965), 159–64.

13 SIMMS, H. H. "A Critical Analysis of Abolition Literature, 1830–1840." *JSH*, VI (1940), 368–82.

14 SLABEY, Robert M. "Joe Christmas, Faulkner's Marginal Man." *Phylon,* XXI (1960), 266–77.

15 TANDY, Jeanette R. See 14.24.

16 TAYLOR, Walter F. "Let My People Go: The White Man's Heritage in *Go Down Moses*." *SAQ*, LVIII (1959), 20–32.

17 TIDWELL, J. N. "Mark Twain's Representation of Negro Speech." *ASp*, XVII (1942), 174–76.

18 TURNER, Arlin. *George W. Cable: A Biography.* Durham, N.C.: Duke UP, 1956.†

19 TURNER, Darwin T. "Daddy Joel Harris and His Old Time Darkies." *SLJ*, I (December, 1968), 20–41.

20 TURNER, Lorenzo Dow. "Walt Whitman and the Negro." *CJF*, XV (1956), 5–11.

21 VICKERY, Olga. *The Novels of William Faulkner.* 2nd ed. Baton Rouge: Louisiana State UP, 1964.

22 WARD, John William. "*Uncle Tom's Cabin*, as a Matter of Historical Fact." *CUF*, IX, i (1966), 42–47.

23 WARFEL, Harry R. "Walt Whitman's *Salut au Monde:* The Ideal of Human Brotherhood." *Phylon*, XIX (1958), 154–56.

24 WARREN, Robert Penn. "Faulkner: The South and the Negro." *SoR*, n.s., I (1965), 501–27.

1 WARREN, Robert Penn. "William Faulkner." *Selected Essays*. New York: Random, 1958.

2 WILSON, Edmund. "'No! No! No! My Soul An't Yours, Mas'r!'" *New Yorker*, XXIV (November 27, 1948), 134–41.

3 WILSON, Edmund. *Patriotic Gore: Studies in the Literature of the American Civil War*. New York: Oxford UP, 1962.†

4 WILSON, Edmund. "William Faulkner's Reply to the Civil-Rights Program." *A Literary Chronicle: 1920–1950*. New York: Doubleday, 1956.

5 WILSON, J. S. "Poor White and Negro." *VQR*, VIII (1932), 621–24.

6 WOODSON, Carter G. "Some Attitudes in English Literature." *JNH*, XX (1935), 27–85.

7 ZANGER, Jules. "The 'Tragic Octoroon' in Pre-Civil War Fiction." *AQ*, XVIII (1966), 63–70.

8 ZIRKER, Priscilla Allen. "Evidence of the Slavery Dilemma in *White Jacket*." *AQ*, XVIII (1966), 477–92.

NOTES

INDEX

INDEX

INDEX

INDEX

Supplement

Currently, articles and books are being published about Afro-American history and culture at a rate which makes it impossible for a bibliographer to keep pace or to anticipate the flood of materials which will appear between preparation and publication of his bibliography. Many publishing companies are producing clothbound or paperback reprints of volumes included in this bibliography. Particular attention should be given to the following reprint series:

The American Negro: His History and Literature. New York: Arno Press and The New York Times.

The Basic Afro-American Reprint Library. New York: Johnson Reprint Corp.

The Black Experience in America. New York: Negro Universities Press.

Black Studies Program in Reprint: Literature of the Black Experience. New York: AMS Press.

Studies in American Negro Life. New York: Atheneum Press.

In addition, Collier is reprinting several valuable literary works; Mnemosyne Press of Miami, Florida, is reprinting books from the Afro-American collections at Fisk University; Bobbs-Merrill of Indianapolis is reprinting essays in the history and criticism of Afro-American literature; and the 3M Corporation is microfilming the very valuable Schomburg Collection of the New York Public Library.

The following are some of the more significant recently published materials which came to the attention of the bibliographer after the manuscript was prepared for publication.

Aids to Research

Bibliographies

1 ABRASH, Barbara. *Black African Literature in English Since 1952.* New York: Johnson Reprint Corp., 1967.

2 JACKSON, Miles M., comp. and ed. *A Bibliography of Negro History and Culture.* Pittsburgh: U of Pittsburgh P, 1969.

3 ROWELL, Charles H. "A Bibliography of Bibliographies for the Study of Black American Literature and Folklore." *Black Experience, A Southern University Journal*, LV (June, 1969), 95–111.

4 RUBIN, Louis D., Jr. *A Bibliographical Guide to the Study of Southern Literature*. Baton Rouge: Louisiana State UP, 1969. (Includes Chesnutt, Ellison, Toomer, Wright.)

5 WOODRESS, James, ed. *American Literary Scholarship: An Annual/1966*. Durham: Duke UP, 1968.

6 WOODRESS, James, ed. *American Literary Scholarship: An Annual/1967*. Durham: Duke UP, 1969.

Significant New Periodicals

7 *The Black Scholar*, Journal of Black Studies and Research. Box 31245, San Francisco.

8 *Black Theatre*. New York: New Lafayette Theatre.

Backgrounds

Slave Narratives

9 BONTEMPS, Arna, ed. *Great Slave Narratives*. New York: Macmillan, 1969. (Autobiographies of Gustavus Vassa, James W. C. Pennington, and William and Ellen Craft.)

10 DREW, Benjamin. *A Northside View of Slavery*. Reading, Mass.: Addison-Wesley, 1969. (Orig. pub. 1855.)

11 LESTER, Julius, ed. *To Be a Slave*. New York: Dial, 1969. (For children.)

12 MONTEJO, Esteban. *The Autobiography of a Runaway Slave*. New York: Pantheon, 1968.

13 OSOFSKY, Gilbert, ed. *Puttin' on Ole Massa*. New York: Harper, 1969. (Narratives of Henry Bibb, William Wells Brown, and Solomon Northrup.)

14 STEWARD, Austin. *Twenty-two Years a Slave and Forty Years a Freeman*. Reading, Mass.: Addison-Wesley, 1969. (Orig. pub. 1857.)

Historical, Social, and Intellectual Backgrounds

15 ADLER, Mortimer J., Charles VAN DOREN, and George DUCAS. *The Negro in American History*. 3 vols. New York: Encyclopedia Britannica, 1969.

16 BENNETT, Lerone, Jr. *Pioneers in Protest.* Chicago: Johnson, 1969.

17 *Black Heroes in World History: Biographies from Tuesday Magazine.* New York: Bantam, 1969. (Includes A. Dumas, P. L. Dunbar, P. Wheatley, *et al.*)

18 CRUSE, Harold. *Rebellion or Revolution.* New York: Morrow, 1968.

19 DAVIDSON, Basil. *Africa in History.* New York: Macmillan, 1969.

20 FANON, Frantz. *The Wretched of the Earth.* New York: Grove, 1968.*†

21 GOLDSTON, Robert. *The Negro Revolution.* New York: Signet, 1969.†

22 GRANT, Joanne. *Confrontation on Campus: The Columbia Pattern of the New Protest.* New York: Signet, 1969.†

23 HARRIS, Janet and Julius HOBSON. *Black Pride.* New York: McGraw-Hill, 1969.

24 KAISER, Ernest. "The Crisis of the Negro Intellectual." *Freedomways,* IX (1969), 24–41.

25 KATZ, William L. *Teachers' Guide to American Negro History.* Chicago: Quadrangle, 1968.

26 MARINE, Gene. *The Black Panthers.* New York: New American Library, 1969.†

27 MILLER, William R. *Martin Luther King, Jr.: His Life, Martyrdom and Meaning for the World.* New York: Weybright and Talley, 1968.

28 MUSE, Benjamin. *The American Negro Revolution: From Non-violence to Black Power, 1963–1967.* Bloomington: Indiana UP, 1969.

29 OSOFSKY, Gilbert. *The Burden of Race.* New York: Harper, 1969.

30 QUARLES, Benjamin. *Black Abolitionists.* New York: Oxford UP, 1969.*

31 ROBINSON, Armstead L., Craig C. FOSTER, and Donald H. OGILVIE, eds. *Black Studies in the University: A Symposium* New Haven: Yale UP, 1969.

32 ROMERO, Pat. *In Black America.* Washington, D.C.: United Pub., 1969.†

33 STONE, Chuck. *Black Political Power in America.* Indianapolis: Bobbs-Merrill, 1968.

34 TEAGUE, Bob. *Letters to a Black Boy.* New York: Lancer, 1969.†

35 TURNER, Lorenzo D. *Africanisms in the Gullah Dialect.* New York: Arno, 1970. (Orig. pub., 1949.)

Art, Journalism, Music, Theatre

36 ARNEZ, Nancy L. and Clara B. ANTHONY. "Contemporary Negro Humor as Social Satire." *Phylon,* XXIX (1968), 339–346.

37 CARAWAN, Guy and Candie, eds. *Freedom Is a Constant Struggle: Songs of the Freedom Movement.* New York: Oak, 1968.

38 CRIPPS, Thomas R. "Movies in the Ghetto, B. P. (Before Poitier)" *ND,* XVIII (Feb., 1969) 21–27, 45–48.

39 GAYLE, Addison, Jr., ed. *Black Expression: Essays by and About Black Americans in the Creative Arts.* New York: Weybright and Talley, 1969.*†

40 TURNER, Sherry. "An Overview of the New Black Arts." *Freedomways,* IX (1969), 156–163.

41 WILLIAMS, Jim. "Pieces on Black Theatre and the Black Theatre Worker." *Freedomways,* IX (1969), 146–155.

Literary History and Criticism

Anthologies

42 MAJOR, Clarence, ed. *The New Black Poetry.* New York: International, 1969.†

43 SCHULBERG, Budd. *From the Ashes.* Cleveland: World, 1969.†

General History and Criticism

44 BARAKA, Ameer (LeRoi Jones). "The Black Aesthetic." *ND,* XVIII (September, 1969), 5–6.

45 CHAMETZKY, Jules and Sidney KAPLAN, eds. *Black and White in American Culture: An Anthology from the Massachusetts Review.* Amherst: U of Massachusetts P, 1969.

46 CARTEY, Wilfred. *Whispers from a Continent: The Literature of Contemporary Black Africa.* New York: Vintage, 1969.*†

47 COOK, Mercer and Stephen HENDERSON. *The Militant Black Writer in Africa and the United States.* Madison: U of Wisconsin P, 1969.

48 EMANUEL, James A. "Black Writers' Views: America Before 1950." *ND,* XVIII (August, 1969), 26–34, 67–69.

49 EVANS, Mari. "I'm With You." *ND,* XVII (May, 1968), 31–36, 77–80.

50 FABIO, Sarah Webster. "A Black Paper." *ND,* XVIII (July, 1969), 26–31.

51 GAYLE, Addison, Jr. See 39.

52 GAYLE, Addison, Jr. "Black Literature and White Aesthetic." *ND,* XVIII (July, 1969), 32–39.

53 GAYLE, Addison, Jr. "Perhaps Not So Soon One Morning." *Phylon*, XXIX (1968), 396–402.

54 GROSS, Theodore L. "Our Mutual Estate: The Literature of the American Negro." *AR*, XXVIII (1968), 293–303.

55 HILL, Herbert. "The Negro Writer and the Creative Imagination." *Arts in Society* (U of Wis.), V (1968), 245–55. (On R. Wright, LeRoi Jones, Ellison, *et al.*)

56 JAHN, Janheinz. *Neo-African Literature: A History of Black Writing.* New York: Grove, 1968.*

57 KILGORE, James C. "The Case for Black Literature." *ND*, XVIII (July, 1969), 22–25, 66–69.

58 SCOTT, Nathan A., Jr. "Judgment Marked by a Cellar: The American Negro Writer and the Dialect of Despair." *U of Denver Quarterly*, II (1967), 5–35.*

59 SCOTT, Nathan A., Jr. *Negative Capability: Studies in the New Literature and the Religious Situation.* New Haven: Yale UP, 1969.

60 TEER, Barbara Ann. "To Black Artists, With Love." *ND*, XVIII (April, 1969), 4–8.

Drama

61 ABRAMSON, Doris E. *Negro Playwrights in the American Theatre, 1925–1959.* New York: Columbia UP, 1969.

62 "Books and Articles Related to Black Theatre Published from 1/1960 to 2/1968." *TDR*, XII (Summer, 1968), 176–80.

63 DIXON, Melvin. "Black Theater: The Aesthetics." *ND*, XVIII (July, 1969), 41–44.

64 KING, Woodie, Jr. "Black Theatre: Present Condition." *TDR*, XII (Summer, 1968), 117–24.

65 MILLER, Adam D. "It's a Long Way to St. Louis: Notes on the Audience for Black Drama." *TDR*, XII (Summer, 1968), 147–50.

66 NEAL, Larry. "The Black Arts Movement." *TDR*, XII (Summer, 1968), 29–39.

67 SILVERA, Frank. "Towards a Theater of Understanding." *ND*, XVIII (April, 1969), 33–35.

Fiction

68 RAMSARAN, J. A. "The Social Groundwork of Politics in Some West Indian Novels." *ND*, XVIII (August, 1969), 71–77.

Poetry

69 CARTEY, Wilfred. "Four Shadows of Harlem." *ND*, XVIII (August, 1969), 22–25.

70 RODGERS, Carolyn M. "Black Poetry—Where It's At." *ND*, XVIII (September, 1969), 7–16.*

Folklore

71 JONES, Bessie. "A Descriptive and Analytical Study of the American Negro Folklore." Nashville: George Peabody Coll, 1968. (Unpublished dissertation.)

Afro-American Writers

Anderson, Alston

72 *All God's Children.* Indianapolis: Bobbs-Merrill, 1965. (Novel.)

Atkins, Russell

73 *Heretofore.* London: Breman, 1969. (Poetry.)

Baldwin, James

74 *The Amen Corner.* New York: Dial, 1968. (Drama.)

BIBLIOGRAPHY AND CRITICISM

75 HOWE, Irving. "James Baldwin: At Ease in Apocalypse." *Harper's*, CCXXXVII (September, 1968), 92–100.

76 PHILLIPS, Louis. "The Novelist As Playwright: Baldwin, McCullers, and Bellow." *Modern American Drama: Essays in Criticism.* Ed. William E. Taylor. Deland, Fla.: Edwards, 1968, pp. 145–162.

Bates, Arthenia

77 *Seeds Beneath the Snow.* New York: Greenwich, 1968. (Stories.)

Brown, William Wells

BIOGRAPHY AND CRITICISM

78 FARRISON, W. Edward. *William Wells Brown: Author and Reformer.* Chicago: U of Chicago P, 1969.*

Bullins, Ed

79 *How Do You Do?* California: Illuminations Press, 1969. (Drama.)

80 *Five Plays.* Indianapolis: Bobbs-Merrill, 1969.

Chesnutt, Charles W.

BIBLIOGRAPHY, BIOGRAPHY, AND CRITICISM

81 GARTNER, Carol B. "Charles W. Chesnutt: Novelist of a Cause." *Markham Review*, III (1968), 5–12.

82 MASON, Julian D., Jr. "Charles W. Chesnutt." See 4, pp. 171–172.

83 KELLER, Kean H. "Charles Waddell Chesnutt (1858–1932)." *American Literary Realism, 1870–1910*, III (1968), 1–4. (Bibliography.)

84 TURNER, Darwin T. "Introduction." *The House Behind the Cedars.* New York: Collier, 1969.†

Cleaver, Eldridge

85 *Post-Prison Writings and Speeches.* New York: Random House, 1969. (Essays).

Cruz, Victor Hernandez

86 *Snaps.* New York: Vintage, 1969. (Poetry.)

DuBois, W. E. B.

BIOGRAPHY AND CRITICISM

87 HARDING, Vincent. "W. E. B. DuBois and the Black Messianic Vision." *Freedomways*, IX (1969), 44–58.*

88 KOSTELANETZ, Richard. "Fictions for a Negro Politics: The Neglected Novels of W. E. B. DuBois." *XUS*, VII (1968), 5–39.

Dunbar, Paul Laurence

BIOGRAPHY AND CRITICISM

89 LARSON, Charles R. "The Novels of Paul Laurence Dunbar." *Phylon*, XXIX (1968), 257–271.

90 TURNER, Darwin T. "Preface." *Lyrics of Lowly Life*. New York: Arno Press and New York Times, 1969.

91 TURNER, Darwin T. "Preface." *The Strength of Gideon and Other Stories*. New York: Arno Press and New York Times, 1969.

Ebon (Thomas Dooley)

92 *Revolution*. Chicago: Third World P, 1969. (Poetry.)

Elder, Lonne

93 *Ceremonies in Dark Old Men*. New York: Farrar, Straus & Giroux, 1969. (Drama.)

Ellison, Ralph

BIBLIOGRAPHY AND CRITICISM

94 SCHAFER, William J. "Ralph Ellison and the Birth of the Anti-Hero." *Critique: Studies in Modern Fiction*, X (1968), 81–93.

95 TISCHLER, Nancy M. "Ralph Ellison." See 4, pp. 191–192.

Evans, Mari

96 *Where Is All the Music?* London: Breman, 1968. (Poetry.)

Fabio, Sarah

97 *A Mirror: A Soul, A Two-Part Volume of Poems.* San Francisco: Richardson, 1969.

Giovanni, Nikki

98 *Black Judgement.* Detroit: Broadside, 1969. (Poetry.)

Heard, Calvin C.

99 *Howard Street.* New York: Dial, 1968. (Novel.)

Hercules, Frank

100 *I Want a Black Doll.* New York: Simon and Schuster, 1967. (Novel.)

Hughes, Langston

BIOGRAPHY AND CRITICISM

101 CARTEY, Wilfred. See 69.

102 DIAKHATÉ, Lamune. "Langston Hughes, conquérant de l'espoir. *PA*, LXIV (1967), 38–46.

103 JONES, Eldred. " 'Laughing to Keep from Crying': a Tribute to Langston Hughes." *PA*, LXIV (1967), 51–55.

104 KING, Woodie, Jr. "Remembering Langston Hughes." *ND*, XVIII (April, 1969), 27–32.

105 KRAMER, Aaron. "Robert Burns and Langston Hughes." *Freedomways*, VIII (1968), 159–66.

106 RIVE, Richard. "Taos in Harlem: An Interview with Langston Hughes." *Contrast*, XIV (1967), 33–39.

Hunter, Kristin

107   *The Soul Brothers and Sister Lou.* New York: Scribner's Sons, 1968. (Fiction for teenagers.)

Johnson, James Weldon

BIOGRAPHY AND CRITICISM

108   JACKSON, Miles M. "Letters to a Friend: Correspondence from James Weldon Johnson to James A. Townes." *Phylon,* XXIX (1968), 182–198.

Jones, LeRoi (Ameer Baraka)

109   COSTELLO, Donald B. "LeRoi Jones: Black Man as Victim. *Commonweal,* LXXXVIII (June 28, 1968), 436–40.

110   JACKSON, Kathryn. "LeRoi Jones and the New Black Writers of the Sixties." *Freedomways,* IX (1969), 232–248.

111   MOOTRY, Maria K. "Themes and Symbols in Two LeRoi Jones Plays." *ND,* XVIII (April, 1969), 42–47.

112   NELSON, Hugh. "LeRoi Jones' *Dutchman:* A Brief Ride on a Doomed Ship." *ETJ,* XX (Feb., 1968), 53–59.

Latimore, Jewel C. (Johari Amini)

113   *Black Essence.* Chicago: Third World P, 1968. (Poetry.)

Lee, Don L.

114   *Don't Cry, Scream!* Detroit: Broadside, 1969. (Poetry.)

McKay, Claude

CRITICISM

115   CARTEY, Wilfred. See 69.

Major, Clarence

116   *All-Night Visitors.* New York: Olympia, 1969. (Novel.)

Marvin X

117   *Black Man, Listen!* Detroit: Broadside, 1969. (Poetry.)

Murphy, Beatrice

118   (With Nancy L. Arnez.) *Home Is Where the Heart Is.* Detroit: Broadside, 1969. (Poetry.)

Neal, Larry

119   *Black Boogaloo* (*Notes on Black Literature*). San Francisco: Journal of Black Poetry P, 1969. (Poetry.)

Reed, Ishmael

120   *Yellow Back Radio Broke-Down.* Garden City: Doubleday, 1969. (Novel.)

Rollins, Bryant

121   *Danger Song.* Garden City: Doubleday, 1967. (Novel.)

Sanchez, Sonia

122   *Homecoming.* Detroit: Broadside, 1969. (Poetry.)

Saunders, Rubie

123   *Marilyn Morgan, R N.* New York: New American Library, 1969. (Novel for teenagers.)

Toomer, Jean

BIBLIOGRAPHY, BIOGRAPHY, AND CRITICISM

124 DILLARD, Mabel. "Jean Toomer: Herald of the Negro Renaissance." Athens: Ohio University, 1967. (Unpublished dissertation.)

125 TURNER, Darwin T. "Jean Toomer." See 4, pp. 311–312.

Williams, John A.

126 *Sons of Darkness, Sons of Light.* Boston: Little, Brown, 1969. (Novel.)

Wright, Richard

127 BRYER, Jackson R. "Richard Wright." See 4, pp. 333–334.

128 Gibson, Donald B. "Richard Wright and the Tyranny of Convention." *CLAJ*, XII (1968), 344–357.

129 GIBSON, Donald B. "Richard Wright: A Bibliographical Essay." *CLAJ.* XII (1968), 360–365.

130 JACKSON, Blyden. "Black Boy from America's Black Belt and Urban Ghettos." *CLAJ*, XII (1968), 287–309.

131 KENT, George E. "On the Future Study of Richard Wright." *CLAJ*, XII (1968), 366–370.

132 KENT, George E. "Richard Wright: Blackness and the Adventure of Western Culture." *CLAJ*, XII (1968), 322–343.

133 KINNAMON, Keneth. "Richard Wright's Use of 'Othello' in 'Native Son'." *CLAJ*, XII (1968), 358–359.

134 KNIPP, Thomas, ed. *Richard Wright: Letters to Joe C. Brown.* Kent: Kent State U Lib, 1968.

Wright, Sarah E.

135 *This Child's Gonna Live.* New York: Delacorte, 1969. (Novel.)

Yerby, Frank

136 *Judas, My Brother.* New York: Dial, 1968.

137 *Speak Now: A Modern Novel.* New York: Dial, 1969.

Criticism of Afro-Americans as Characters

138 MOSS, Carlton. "The Great White Hope." *Freedomways*, IX (1969), 127–138.

139 TISCHLER, Nancy M. *Black Masks: Negro Characters in Modern Southern Fiction.* University Park: Pennsylvania State UP, 1969.